The Impact of Experience and Education for Successful Entrepreneurs

by

Dr. Edward L. Wiggins

COPYRIGHT 2016

Author	Edward L. Wiggins, D.B.A.
Publisher	DBC Publishing, Colonial Beach & Gloucester, Virginia
ISBN	978-1948149198
Cover Art	2022© DBC Publishing

This text has been altered in format from the original dissertation to conform to better readability for the general-public and commercial publishing standards. The author may also have updated text, content, added more resources and bibliography material after the original dissertation was first published. Scholars reviewing the contents and formatting for thesis or dissertation styling should _not_ use this book's current *formatting* as a model. See your educational institution's established dissertation guidelines for the acceptable formatting for the graduate level thesis.

You may contact the author with questions, comments, or continuing research inquiries at: ewiggins@orbisnovitas.com

TABLE OF CONTENTS

LIST OF TABLES

LIST OF FIGURES

ABSTRACT

This qualitative study aims to examine the lived experiences to understand how leadership experience and acquisition of education impact the success of African-American entrepreneurs in Northern Virginia. African-American entrepreneurs have a lower success rate in business than any other ethnic group. Leadership experience and formal and informal education are traits African-American entrepreneurs have direct control over to influence success in business. Unlimited research literature is available on the identified problems for African-American entrepreneurs, but limited research exists with qualitative solutions to these problems.

The sample population for this study involved 21 successful African-American entrepreneurs in Northern Virginia. The qualitative phenomenological research design will utilize unstructured, open-ended questions administered through in-depth interviews. The interviews of these successful African-American entrepreneurs involved understanding their lived experience in relation to business, leadership/management, and the acquisition of education.

The core themes are summarized as follows: (a) motivation, (b) challenges and obstacles, (c) important entrepreneurial characteristics, (d) entrepreneurial advice, (e) leadership background, (f) leadership development, (g) prior business experience, (h) gained business experience, (i) other relevant business experience, (j) formal education, (k) formal education benefits, (l) informal education, (m) informal education benefits.

ACKNOWLEDGEMENTS

I am honored to acknowledge Dr. Grace Klinefelter for being my program and committee chair. Your invaluable guidance and seamless patience made my entire doctoral experience manageable and productive. I express gratitude to my committee members for the knowledge and expertise you provided throughout my dissertation research.

I was fortunate to be graced by the presence of my academic cohort who shared professional and industry knowledge, tutored me through challenging courses, and created a positive environment that nurtured progression toward our common goal. This is definitely an academic journey one does not take alone. The full support of Argosy University's staff (writing lab, student, financial, and academic services) fostered an atmosphere focused on learning and virtually free from administrative distractions as I worked to complete my degree.

I give special thanks to the successful African-American entrepreneurs who took the time from their busy schedules to participate in my research. It is your valuable entrepreneurial insight that incorporate solutions to the existing body of research on what are the executable provisions for African-American entrepreneurs to be successful in the world of business.

DEDICATION

I dedicate this academic work to God, my children, my family, and my closest friends. I give praise to my spiritual father, God, for guiding me down this academic path of growth that inspired so many areas of my life, the strength to endure and overcome the obstacles along my doctoral journey, and the faith to follow through to the end.

I thank my children (Jumiele, Jurney, and Edward N. Wiggins) for being my center node of purpose and guiding light. It is your consistent academic excellence, sacrifice, and patience that inspired me to thrive above and beyond all. I sincerely hope this manuscript and my demonstrated efforts are symbolic to the importance of education as you continue to develop your academic and intellectual capacity. I love you!

I appreciate my family (Mother, Linda Wiggins; Sister, Julanda Sparkman; Brother, Eric Wiggins; and Cousin, Janie Bradley) for being my supporting cast. It is with humility and humbleness I graciously thank you and gratefully honor you with an abundance of love for your foundation of enduring support.

I give special thanks to my other family members … my family is the greatest! Finally, I bestow a tremendous amount of reverence to my closest friends who were my pillars of support. It is through my family and friends' immutable support and corroboration without judgment that allowed my ambitions manifest into reality.

CHAPTER ONE

INTRODUCTION

The purpose of this qualitative study was to examine the lived experiences of African-American entrepreneurs in Northern Virginia to understand how leadership experience and acquisition of formal/informal education impact their success. The sample population for this study involved 21 successful African-American entrepreneurs in Northern Virginia. The results add more depth to the body of existing literature and empower nascent African-American entrepreneurs with formulas for success in leadership experience and formal and informal education.

The African-American population was 13.6% of the United States population in 2010 (U.S. Census Bureau, 2010a). However, African-American entrepreneurs were underrepresented compared to other minority groups and have the lowest (business) survival rate beyond five years (Fairlie & Robb, 2008). The African-American self-employment rate was only 6% compared to the 11.6% self-employment rate of White Americans in 2009 (Hipple, 2010). The 51% difference in the self-employment rate between African Americans and White Americans was historically attributed to the societal problems of racial discrimination and access to capital (Gibson, Harris, Walker, & McDowell, 2014). Research findings from the late 20th century on the paucity of African-American entrepreneurs identified the individual attributes of limited business experience and entrepreneurial knowledge as supplementary contributors (Bogan & Darity, 2008; Fairlie & Robb, 2008; Kinion, 2012; Robinson, 2014; Smith & Tang, 2013).

African-American entrepreneurs proliferated in the 21st century despite the well-documented history of business failure. The Panel Study of Entrepreneurial Dynamics (PSED) assessments found African-American men's participation in entrepreneurial endeavors increased by 30% and was traceable to the attainment of higher education (Reynolds & Curtin, 2008). The initial PSED I assessment was conducted in 1999 and was succeeded by the PSED II assessment in 2005. African-American college graduates were 1.79 times more likely to become nascent (budding) entrepreneurs in comparison to White counterparts with comparable educational background(s) (Lofstrom & Bates, 2013; Parker, 2009). These figures illustrate African Americans are actively engaged in self-employment. Additional qualitative research will contribute to a more in-depth understanding of successful African-American entrepreneurs.

Problem Background

African-American entrepreneurs had (2016) a lower success rate in business than any other ethnic group. The reasons cited for limited business success of African-American entrepreneurs encompass racial discrimination (Ahn, 2011; Davidson, Fielden, & Omar, 2010; Robinson, 2014), access to capital (Blanchflower, Levine, & Zimmerman, 2003; Cavalluzzo & Wolken, 2005; Fairlie & Robb, 2007; Smith & Tang, 2013), lack of business experience (DeCaro, DeCaro, & Bowen-

Thompson, 2010; Kinion, 2012; Sheppard, 2010) and limited entrepreneurial knowledge (Alexander, 2013; Lofstrom & Bates, 2013; Parker, 2009; Singh, & Gibbs, 2013). Racial discrimination is the overarching societal paradigm that inhibits equitable development of “economic, political, educational, and social opportunities” for African Americans and other minorities (National Association of School Psychologists, 2012, p.1).

The African-American community has been exposed to these inherent inequalities of racial discrimination for centuries (Benton, 2012; Equal Justice Initiative, 2014). The lack of access to capital, limited business experience, and entrepreneurial knowledge are byproducts from centuries of racial discrimination (National Association of Social Workers, 2015). The quality of resources for education, housing, healthcare, and employment were significantly lower in urban environments as compared to suburban environments (National Association of Social Workers, 2015). The social impact of racism manifested through education, economic, political, and social inequalities that hindered the advancement of African-American businesses for over four centuries. These impacts were well-demonstrated through the mainstream environmental settings of African Americans, presented through government statistics of unemployment rate, self-employment success, and education attainment. Therefore, the examples of constructive life lessons and positive role models were exceptionally diminished in an environment plagued by inadequate resources derived from discrimination.

Historical research on African-American entrepreneurs' limited business success revealed two consistent themes: pronounced racial discrimination and the lack of access to capital (Gibson, et al., 2014; Lough, 2015; McDonald-Warren, 2010). In 1958, the Small Business Administration (SBA) established minority disadvantage programs to reduce the inequalities from racial discrimination and increase access to capital. Minority small businesses' start-up and survival rates decreased, which contradicted the U.S. government's anticipated resolution to the problem. According to Bogan and Darity (2008), the African-American, self-employment rate decreased between 1960 and 1990. Subsequently, new studies were conducted to identify the circumstances that contributed to the decline in minority-owned businesses after initiation of the minority disadvantage business programs. By the late 20th century, research findings on the number of African-American entrepreneurs introduced new evidence on the lack of experience and education that hindered business development and progression. This evidence was traceable to the African-American entrepreneur's individual traits: business experience and entrepreneurial knowledge (Bogan & Darity, 2008; Fairlie & Robb, 2008; Kinion, 2012; Smith & Tang, 2013). African-American entrepreneurs recognized some progress in the 21st century in spite of the identified business trait limitations.

In the 21st century, the number of African-American professionals with college degrees increased along with the development of stronger business traits (Banks, 2012). African-American professionals with academic degrees and technical certifications have stronger business traits and are more competitive for top-level business positions. Nevertheless, there still are difficulties with qualified African Americans achieving top-level positions.

Brown (2014) indicated African-American professionals were more likely to be employed as a mediator handling minorities (i.e., clients and/or communities) for corporate/government. or serving in an affirmative action-defined position. African-American professionals had become increasingly dissatisfied working as an employee due to these disparities within the workforce (Alexander, 2013). The disparities were the levels of inequality on performance evaluations for promotion, career advancement, mentorship, enforcement of Equal Employment Opportunity (EEO) regulations and directives, and training and development assignments continually discouraging African-American professionals in corporate and government positions (Brown, 2014; Harper-Anderson, 2008; Momah, 2011; U.S. Equal Employment Opportunity Commission, 2010).

The pursuit of entrepreneurship became a viable alternative to working as an employee (Griffith, 2013; Latha & Murthy, 2009). African-American professionals sought more control over job satisfaction, career advancements, and economic independence through entrepreneurship. Although the transition from employee to entrepreneur can be a complex process, these discriminatory practices inspire African-American professionals to transition into entrepreneurship for personal satisfaction and professional control.

There are African Americans who have established successful businesses in spite of the centuries of discrimination, which led to the social impacts of access to capital, limited business experience, and entrepreneurial knowledge. Banks (2012) asserted that African-American entrepreneurs' ownership and success had increased in fields with previously low involvement. These fields required highly educated and skill-intensive expertise like professional services, business, and finance. Minimal research exists with evidence on the proven business characteristics traits and practices of these successful African-American entrepreneurs.

Purpose of the Study

The purpose of this study was to gain an in-depth understanding of successful African-American entrepreneurs' lived experiences by conducting a qualitative analysis to evaluate the impact of leadership experience and formal and informal education have on business success. Leadership experience and formal and informal education are traits, which African-American entrepreneurs have direct control over to influence their success in business. Unlimited research literature is available on identified problems for African-American entrepreneurs, but limited research existed (in 2016) that correlated qualitative solutions to these identified problems.

The identified problems are only part of the equation in the problem-solving process. There are resources available with a variety of problem-solving models, and each model has following fundamental elements: problem – identify/define, solution – analyze/implement, and evaluation – review/revise (Department of the Army, 2010; Isaksen, Dorval, & Treffinger, 2011; Restructuring Associates, 2008). More qualitative studies are needed to present a plausible solution for the well-documented problems that impede the success of African-American entrepreneurs.

Research Questions

Research Question 1 (RQ1): What are the lived leadership experiences of successful African-American entrepreneurs providing professional, scientific, and technical services in Northern Virginia?

Entrepreneurial leadership experience is the proficiency to methodically identify potential business risks and efficiently mitigate the "various challenges of new venture creation and thereby increase the probability of their success in the business world" (Bagheri & Pihie, 2011, p. 449). Leadership incorporates management for this research. Leadership and management are intrinsically linked from a small business perspective because an entrepreneur can be responsible for leadership and management in a new or small business venture. However, leadership and management have distinctive meanings. Leadership involves dealing with change, vision, strategies, and innovation, while management maintains the infrastructure that monitors and controls operational consistency (Bontas, 2012).

Research Question 2 (RQ2): What are the experiences of acquiring formal and informal education in relation to successful African-American entrepreneurs providing professional, scientific, and technical services in Northern Virginia?

Education is the process of acquiring knowledge; the acquisition of knowledge can be obtained through formal or informal methods (Zafar & Khan, 2014). Education is a term that incorporates training and knowledge acquisition for this research. Formal education and training acquired through infrastructures validate a level of proficiency. An accredited college or certified training institution can be a formal education infrastructure, whereas informal education does not have organized accreditation or certification curricula. Knowledge acquired from informal education to update an individual's knowledge base can be sourced through auto-didacticism for instance seminars, professional literature, the Internet, and scientific or didactic games (Zafar & Khan, 2014).

Definition of Terms

The following definitions provide clarity for interpretation and understanding of the terms for this research:

African-American: A person (i.e., male or female) born and raised in the United States; African American/Black alone or in combination with other races as defined by the U.S. Census Bureau (2010a).

Developing Nation: Known as newly industrialized countries (e.g., India, Brazil, China, and Mexico) with an underdeveloped industrial base and a low Gross Domestic Product (GDP) per capita relative to developed countries (e.g., Australia, Canada, United Kingdom, and the United States).

Economic Class System: The social class structure or socio-economic system that separates the workforce into three categories based on income, education, and type of occupation: upper, middle, and lower class. Income status is the most measured variable.

Education: Used interchangeably with entrepreneurial knowledge. The process of acquiring knowledge through formal or informal methods (Zafar & Khan, 2014).

Entrepreneurial Leadership Experience: Used interchangeably with business experience and management experience. The proficiencies to methodically identify potential business risk and efficiently mitigate the "various challenges of new venture creation and thereby increase the probability of their success in the business world" (Bagheri & Pihie, 2011, p. 449).

Formal Education: Acquired through infrastructures that validate a level of proficiency. A formal education infrastructure can be an accredited college or certified training institution (Zafar & Khan, 2014).

Hourglass Economy: A visual representation and definition of economic inequality that produces more upper and lower classes, causing a decline in the middle class.

Informal Education: Informal education does not have organized accreditation or certification curricula. Knowledge acquired from informal education can be sourced through the conventional means of seminars, professional literature, the Internet, and other practical applications (i.e., scientific or didactic games, lectures, case studies, discussions) to update your knowledge base (Mwasalwiba, 2010; Rih & Guedira, 2014; Zafar & Khan, 2014).

Leadership: Involves dealing with change, vision, strategies, and innovation of an entity (Bontas, 2012).

Management: The act of maintaining the infrastructure that monitors and controls operational consistency within an entity (Bontas, 2012).

Northern Virginia: Incorporates the cities and towns of Alexandria, Arlington, Centerville, Culpeper, Dulles, Falls Church, Fairfax, Fredericksburg, Herndon, Leesburg, Manassas, Manassas Park, McLean, Occoquan, Reston, Spotsylvania, Springfield, Triangle, Vienna, Warrenton, and Woodbridge. This area includes the counties of Caroline, Fauquier, Loudoun, Prince William, Rappahannock, and Stafford (Commonwealth of Virginia, 2015).

Successful Small Business Entrepreneur: The Small Business Administration (2014) asserts the following criteria:

1. a full-time business owner who has been an entrepreneur for a minimum of five (5) years,
2. less than 500 employees,
3. must be active in the decision-making of the daily business management and operations, and
4. hold 51% or more of the stock or equity in the business.

White American: A person having origins in any of the original peoples of Europe, the Middle East, or North Africa as defined by the U.S. Census Bureau (2010b). Alternatively referred to as European American or Caucasian (non-Hispanic).

Significance of the Study

The significance of this research study will improve the intellectual capital of African-American entrepreneurs, thereby encouraging economic empowerment and self-sufficiency. Leadership experience and entrepreneurial knowledge are essential attributes that increase business acumen for nascent African-American entrepreneurs. African-American entrepreneurs traditionally do not have the support of historical family business experience, entrepreneur support infrastructure, or network system to recognize, analyze, and cultivate business opportunities (Fairlie & Robb, 2008). Therefore, prospective African-American entrepreneurs must have or develop self-reliance and insight to identify and evaluate legitimate (i.e., logical, realistic, and profitable) business opportunities. Aside from the financial obstacle (e.g., financing or funding the business startup), the entrepreneur must have the ability to recognize business opportunities as vital in the entrepreneurial process.

Education and business management experience are intangible qualification factors categorized under the business-owner's characteristics, which lenders use to determine the level of risk associated with a financial loan (Pattie, Parks, & Wales, 2012). Lenders evaluate a business owner's character (e.g., business or industry experience, education level, relationship with lender/lender institution, and professional references) as intangible qualifications in addition to the traditional qualification factors of credit history, cash flow, and business or personal collateral (Arora, 2014; Biz Filings, 2012; Small Business Notes, 2015). An increase in business experience will positively influence the performance rating, and the educational improvements will increase the human-capital consideration of entrepreneurs. The proactive approach of African-American entrepreneurs to eliminate the constraints of limited business experience and knowledge will ultimately increase the potential for approved minority-owned business loans, initial or expanded lines of credit, and reduced interest rates.

Bone Research (2014) suggests minorities still experience remnants of discrimination despite having the same qualifications as their White (Caucasian, non-Hispanic) counterparts when applying for business loans. African Americans and other minorities can indirectly combat discrimination (i.e., societal problems) by meeting or exceeding the measurable qualifications (e.g., business experience and entrepreneurial knowledge). The lending institutions would be in jeopardy of legal actions under the Equal Credit Opportunity Act of 1974 if challenged with substantiated evidence of comparable qualifications which warranted approved business loans, increased lines of credit, or reduced interest rates.

The African-American unemployment rate had been consistently 50% higher than the national unemployment rate for the past 50 years in the United States (Singh & Gibbs, 2013). The United States has experienced an unemployment rate of 7.9%, while the African-American population endured an unemployment rate of 16.7% during the global financial crisis in 2007 (U.S. Bureau of Labor Statistics, 2014). Additionally, the unemployment rate of African-American college graduates was 11.9% in 2013, which is relatively high compared to White (Caucasian; non-Hispanic) college graduates at 8% (Shierholz, Sabadish, & Finio, 2013). The extensive corporate downsizing and the global financial crisis between 2007 – 2009 encouraged the next generation of workers to explore entrepreneurship to generate primary or secondary income.

Another income avenue considered a worthwhile endeavor to avoid unemployment is free enterprise. College students and graduates view entrepreneurship as a viable career option after being unable to obtain employment or witnessing relatives become unemployed from corporate downsizing (Scarborough, 2012). Entrepreneurship within the African-American community is becoming more of a survival necessity versus a casual endeavor (Carter, 2014). There is a need to explore a deeper understanding of successful African-American's leadership and education experience for entrepreneurial progression.

A successful business venture is weighed on a variety of external and internal factors to the environment (Jain, Trehan, & Trehan, 2010). Externally, there are legal considerations (e.g., taxes and employee health benefits, and international business laws) and the changing dynamics of the economy shifting to a globalized market (Mason, 2012). Internally, the inability to control financial capital, manage organizations, resolve business problems, and strategically plan for growth and market changes was consistently cited for African-

American entrepreneurs' start-up failures (Brown, 2014).

There are other contributing internal factors considered with respect to African-American business owners' success. Entrepreneurs with a college-level education had an increased probability of surviving and growing in the business. According to Sonfield and Lussier (2014), more education acquired for a business discipline improves entrepreneurial strategies to realize opportunities with more innovation and less risk. Education contributes to the entrepreneur's analytical aptitude to recognize and synthesize business opportunities (Singh & Gibbs, 2013).

The Northern Virginia area was rated number four among the "best places for black-owned businesses" (Todd, 2015, p. 1). Northern Virginia, including Washington, DC, consists of 18% black-owned businesses, and of those, 6% consisted of paid employees (Todd, 2015). The Northern Virginia metropolitan area was a leader in the Department of Defense (DOD) contracts (Badenhausen, 2013). Moreover, other industries that stimulated the local economy were bioscience, logistics, manufacturing, and technology (Badenhausen, 2013). Northern Virginia was enriched with business opportunities that required well-managed businesses with a highly educated workforce to meet these economic demands.

CHAPTER TWO

REVIEW OF THE LITERATURE

Scholarly literature was identified, evaluated, and synthesized from a diversity of professions, including business, psychology, social services, and education, to gain a more in-depth understanding of this phenomenon (Fink, 2010). Leadership experience and education were indispensable elements associated with African-American entrepreneurs' success in business (Kinion, 2012; Robinson, 2014; Sheppard, 2010; Smith & Tang, 2013). Entrepreneurs had direct control over these variables to positively influence growth and prosperity in business.

History of African-American Entrepreneurs

A review of literature prior to 1990 presented African-American entrepreneurs' limited business life was due to the consistent theme of insufficient capitalization and the pronounced presence of discrimination (Gibson et al., 2014). Racial discrimination was the center node to other identified factors (e.g., lack of access to capital, limited business experience, and entrepreneurial knowledge) that contributed to African-American entrepreneurs' limited business success. Racism was the ideology of supremacy forced on a group deemed inferior. Racism was the use of power to establish disparities between groups for the simple reasons of differences in race, ethnicity, national origin, or cultural heritage (National Association of Social Workers, 2015). The African-American community had been exposed to these inherent inequalities of racial discrimination for over 400 years.

The social impact of racism has manifested through education, economic, political, and social inequalities that have hindered the development and progress of African Americans for over four centuries. The United States' justification of slavery was the rawest form of racial inequality, denying basic human rights. Africans were originally brought to the United States (U.S.) as enslaved people in 1619, and slavery did not end until the Emancipation Act of 1863

(Benton, 2012; National Archives, 2016). African Americans were further discriminated against by racial segregation after slavery legislatively ended. Racial segregation was legally concluded by the Civil Rights Act of 1964.

Traditionally, discrimination was socially acceptable and openly exercised in public, especially during the Jim Crow Era from the post-Civil War and ended at the inception of the Voting Rights Act in 1968. The Jim Crow Laws were a collection of government statutes, which legalized racial segregation with the objective to marginalize African Americans (Jim Crow Law, 2022). Discrimination remains evident today based on the unemployment, self-employment, income, and education – statistical disparities identified by the U.S. Bureau of Labor Statistics (2014, 2015a, 2015b), U.S. Census Bureau (2007, 2010a), and National Center for Education Statistics (2014).

Today, overt discrimination is more likely to lurk behind the scenes to avoid the nearly instantaneous retaliation from social media, which delivers judgment from a global perspective. Modern-day discrimination has evolved into closeted surreptitious societies acting as the gatekeepers of the glass ceiling, an invisible barrier denying minorities access to achievements in the world of business (Johns, 2013).

The U.S. government created programs, laws, and policies to establish a level of equality. Equality initiatives were executed under the Small Business Administration (SBA) programs (e.g., Management and Technical Assistance Program and Business Development Program), established to help African American and other minority entrepreneurs leverage business opportunities and provide access to capital. The legislative changes provided lending support, tax incentives, and other critical resources for small businesses (U.S. Government Publishing Office, 2010). The performance of the disadvantaged minority programs under SBA was not strongly effective with increasing the success rate of African-American and other minorities entrepreneurs and other minorities. According to Bogan and Darity (2008), the African-American, self-employment rate decreased between 1960 and 1990. As a result, additional research was executed to investigate the adverse impact on African-American entrepreneurs.

Scholarly research in the late 20th century on African-American entrepreneurs revealed newly identified factors in conjunction with the traditional theme of insufficient capitalization and the pronounced presence of discrimination. The new findings were limited business experience and knowledge. African American entrepreneurial experience and knowledge were hampered by the limited ability to recognize, analyze, and process opportunities effectively weighed against economic realities (Singh & Gibbs, 2013). African-American entrepreneurs tended to base business decisions on optimistic perspectives as opposed to economic realities (Makhbul & Hasun, 2011; Smith & Tang, 2013). These optimistic perspectives were an extension of African Americans' socio-economic, lower-income environments, which did not mirror the U.S. mainstream, socio-economic realities. Researchers proposed a link between higher education and the increased capacity to realize quality opportunities (Ramos-Rodriquez, Medina-Garrido, Lorenzo-Gomez, & Ruiz-Navarro, 2010; Singh, Knox, & Crump, 2008). As a result of these findings, policies, and programs were initiated and updated to bridge the gap in African-American entrepreneurs' business experience and opportunities.

Importance of Successful African-American Entrepreneurs

The social stratification in the United States is generally known as the upper, middle, and lower classes. The income of the socio-economic classes are as follows: 1) Upper Class - $157,000 and above, (19%), 2) Middle Class ranges between $156,000 and $52,000 (52%), and Lower Class is $51,000 and below (29%) (Bennett, Fry, and Kochhar, 2022). The middle class is considered the backbone of the U.S. economy. The U.S. economic structure changed from an industrial workforce 1750 – 1900s (labor-driven) to a technological workforce 1975 – currently (information-driven). Labor-intensive jobs were exported to developing nations in the economic transition due to implement more competitive labor prices. Production costs were cheaper in developing nations, including the costs to export the materials and importing products back to the U.S. for final assembly and sale. During the 2008-2010 Great Recession, there was a 60% decrease in employment for the middle-class workforce, with only a 22% recovery in the years following (National Employment Law Project, 2012). The U.S. middle-class workforce shrunk dramatically, which had a crippling impact on the U.S. socio-economic class, system dynamics.

The Great Recession, globalization, and technology changed the dynamics of the U.S. socio-economic class system in the first decade of the 21st century. The socio-economic class system visually presents an irregular hourglass, which illustrated a reduction in the middle-class workforce and an increase in the upper-class and lower-class workforce (Lansley, 2013; Sission, 2011; Starr, 2012). The following graph in Figure 1 illustrates the reduction of the middle-class families between 1970 – 2008 (Reardon & Bischoff, 2011).

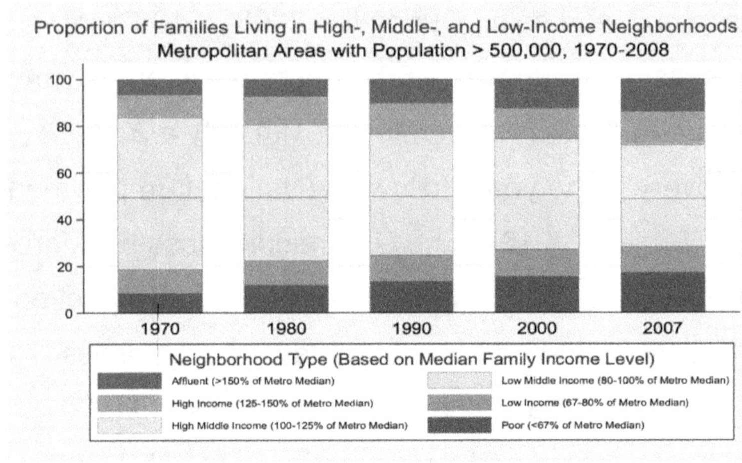

Figure 1 - Proportion of Families by Income Levels

The hourglass effect among the socio-economic class disparity will continue as the demand for technology progresses. The Pew Research Center affirmed a clear trajectory of increasing upper-class wealth, but no wealth growth for the middle and lower class, including a noticeable gap in the ethnic demographics in The Great Recession (Fry & Kochhar, 2014). The middle class moved to either the upper class or lower class in the squeeze of the middle-class workforce.

The viable career options for the middle-class workforce are to transition from manual labor positions into corporate America's professional service positions or entrepreneurship. Griffith (2013) affirmed people were increasingly turning to entrepreneurship due to dwindling opportunities within corporate America. More specifically, African Americans were dissatisfied with the barriers that hindered progression into corporate America. These barriers in the new corporate economy environment were the old boy network (e.g., lack of access to the corporate network); lack of mentors and sponsors; racial stereotyping, cultural and background differences; lack of recruitment; unfair assessments or performance appraisals; radicalized jobs; discrimination, and lack of delegated authority (Harper-Anderson, 2008; Momah, 2011).

In addition, there were barriers (e.g., human capital, financial capital) to overcome in entrepreneurship.

Statistics. The African Americans' self-employment rate was 6% compared to the 11.6% self-employment rate of White Americans in 2009, which is a delta of more than 50% (Hipple, 2010). The African-American population endured an unemployment rate of 16.7%, while the U.S. overall unemployment rate was 7.9% during the global financial crisis in 2007 (U.S. Bureau of Labor

Statistics, 2014). The unemployment rate improved in 2015 with 9.9% for the African-American population and 5.1% for workers overall in the United States (U.S. Bureau of Labor Statistics, 2015a; U.S. Bureau of Labor Statistics, 2015b). However, the 50% delta remained relevant in the unemployment rate comparison. The National Center for Education Statistics (2014) indicated the following details on the African-American population in 2013: (a) the gap in educational attainment increased from 13% to 20%, (b) the highest rate of children living in poverty was 39% (delta of 26% compared to White children), (c) the lowest high school graduation rate of 68% (Asian had the highest rate of 93%), and (d) the next generation was disproportionately three times more likely to live in poverty. In retrospect, there was a prediction of a 13% increase in immediate college enrollment.

Impact. The historically low statistical rates on African-American businesses are well-documented facts published and reported through the U.S. Bureau of Labor Statistics, U.S. Census Bureau, and nonpartisan research organizations (National Center for Education Statistics, 2014; National Employment

Law Project, 2012; Pew Research Center, 2015; Urban Institute, 2017). These reports included data on the cultural and family infrastructure of African Americans. The culture and family background of African Americans had a fundamental effect on the attainment of education and entrepreneurship. African-Americans' education and self-employment disposition were natural corollaries of the cultural and family environment. According to Danes, Lee, Stafford, and Heck (2008), the ethnicity of culture and family dictated the orientation toward the business environment. Traditionally, African Americans were residentially segregated from mainstream society and business environments. The African-American culture developed a myopic view of the economy and business. This to an earlier statement of why African-American entrepreneurs tended to base business decisions on optimistic perspectives as opposed to economic realities (Makhbul & Hasun, 2011; Smith & Tang, 2013).

Consequently, African-American families' high unemployment rate, low household income, and value of assets (e.g., real property, investments) had an impact on whether a child would pursue formal education or graduate with a college degree (Griffith, 2013; Zlomek, 2012). African Americans were culturally limited in family business inheritance, business experience, entrepreneur support infrastructure, or network system to recognize, analyze, and cultivate business opportunities, which were not reflective of conventional business realities. As Fairlie and Robb (2008, p. 298) suggested:

> *The lack of family business experience may contribute substantially to the relative lack of success of black-owned businesses because of limited opportunities to receive the informal learning or apprenticeship-type training that occurs in working in a family business. Family businesses provide an opportunity for family members to acquire general business human capital, and in many cases, they also provided the opportunity for acquiring specific business human capital.*

A majority of the comprehensive statistical resources illustrated entrepreneurs, the self-employed, and business-owners (to include the disadvantaged), on average, earn more and experience faster income growth than hourly-wage-earners or salaried employees. Numerous government programs were available for minority-owned disadvantaged businesses (e.g., loans, set-asides, mentorship). A benefit for African-American entrepreneurs was a human capital investment in self-improvement. This individual investment will inherently influence African-American families and, eventually, the African-American culture.

Theoretical Considerations

Theoretical considerations originated from grounding theories on entrepreneurship, leadership, and education. The theories of entrepreneurship were economic, psychological, and sociological models. The theoretical reflections for leadership were more interwoven with detailing the difference in leadership, management, entrepreneurship, and entrepreneurial leadership. The theories of leadership (e.g., traits, styles, and behavior) referring to how entrepreneurial leadership was incorporated into the leadership framework. The theoretical approach used for education was channeled through the types of knowledge acquisition (formal, informal).

Literature Review

Entrepreneurship

The literature reviewed from the 21st century on African-American entrepreneurs identified human capital (e.g., experience, education, expertise) as an absolute necessity for operating a successful business (Alexander, 2013; DeCaro et al., 2010; Fairlie & Robb, 2007; Kinion, 2012; Lofstrom & Bates, 2013; Parker, 2009; Sheppard, 2010; Singh, & Gibbs, 2013) aside from the financial capital credentials (Blanchflower et al., 2003; Cavalluzzo & Wolken, 2005; Smith & Tang, 2013).

Entrepreneurship was an action-based process for creating a venture with economic market value and was the driving force behind economic development and progression, as acknowledged by scholars and economists (Bosma, Wennekers & Amorós, 2011; Newbold & Erwin, 2014; Taneja, 2010). The entrepreneur's role in the economy was intimately linked to competition, creativity, innovation, economic growth, and job creation by taking a risk in new business ventures to build value in the marketplace (Isenberg, 2013; Mars & Rios-Agilar, 2010; Raposo & do Paço, 2011). Understanding the entrepreneurship phenomena provided depth to the basic description of entrepreneurship and entrepreneur. The theories of entrepreneurship were generally consolidated into the categories of economic, psychological, and sociological perspectives.

Literature dated back to Richard Cantillon in the 16th century was accredited as the origin of the theory of entrepreneurship and was expounded from an economic perspective. Cantillon's entrepreneurship theory was originally an isolated thought in the theoretical analysis of commerce derived from personal experience rather than the constructive foundation for economic theory (Brown & Thornton, 2013).

The economic theory of entrepreneurship was defined as building or purchasing a product at a fixed cost and selling that product at a price greater than the initial investment cost (Brown & Thornton, 2013). The distribution of a product in a competitive market was the model of free trade, which involved the basic components of production (e.g., land, labor, and capital) as pronounced by classical theory scholars (Ricardo, 1817; Say, 1803; & Smith, 1776). In contrast, scholars criticize the classical theory's relativity to production in the neo-classical theory. The neo-classical theory focuses on supply and demand as the driving forces behind the production, pricing, and consumption of goods and services. Knight (1921) and Coarse (1937) argued the economic theory of entrepreneurship did not depend on production as a central node, and classical theory excludes the consideration of entrepreneurial activity. Instead, the neoclassical theory suggested the economic system existed without a central control through the coordination of pure exchange. Goods traded for money or other goods and services was the basis of a pure exchange. The diminishing marginal utility (i.e., a perceived value) combined with exchange generated "enough impetus for entrepreneurship" in the economic system (Simpeh, 2011, p.1).

The psychological theory of entrepreneurship introduced the aspiration for achievement as the drive behind innovative activities (McClelland, 1967). The aspiration for achievement personality traits was a greater degree of tolerance for ambiguity, a higher propensity for taking a risk, and an increased level of autonomy. This type of entrepreneur had an internal locus of control to guide a positive outcome through their behavior and actions (Cuervo, Ribeiro, & Roig, 2007). A study conducted by Cooper and Dunkelberg (1987) confirmed commonalities between 890 entrepreneurs: better educated, parents own/owned a business, started a business related to a previous job, or a business local to their residence. These psychological attributes of entrepreneurs remain relevant in current research despite being challenged by psychologists biased toward successful entrepreneurs. Other psychological theories of entrepreneurship were conducted that produced comparisons to non-entrepreneurs, types of entrepreneurs, and demographic studies (Gartner, 1985; Vesper, 1980).

The sociological theory concentrated on three sub-factors: establishing social relationships, a meaningful life, and ethnic identification (Simpeh, 2011). The social relationship gained people's trust as opposed to opportunism. The meaningful life perspective encouraged others, so actions of positive influence justify life. Ethnic identification involved the social background of an entrepreneur. The social environment was closely related to the ethnic culture. An entrepreneur's cultural inputs (e.g., ethnic, social, economic, ecological, and political) shaped the attitude and behavior (Baskerville, 2003; Mitchell et al., 2002). The culture affects the attitude and behavior of an entrepreneur, which can be either negative or positive.

The economic, psychological, and sociological theory of entrepreneurship demonstrated different perspectives to motivate an entrepreneur. Consequently, the core attributions of an entrepreneur were still indistinguishable. An entrepreneur possessed the defining qualities characterized by autonomy, risk-taking, innovation, pro-activeness, and competitive aggressiveness (Isenberg, 2013; Murad, 2014; Raposo & do Paço, 2011; Sánchez, 2010). These entrepreneurial qualities materialized from the original work of Covin and Slevin (1991) and Lumpkin and Dess (1996).

The entrepreneurial orientation or qualities are inclusive regardless of the theory of entrepreneurship category. A high degree of correlation was noted between entrepreneurial orientation and increased business performance (Xu & Xu, 2012; Yang, 2008). The Xu and Yang's studies specifically indicated pro-activeness and innovativeness with having a statistical significance among the five qualities. Risk-taking was more difficult to measure against performance. Krauss, Frese, Friedrich, & Unger (2005) declared environmental and industry factors were likely to distort the results in the comparison between risk-taking and performance.

Leadership

In modern-day society, leadership and management were viewed as one – or used synonymously in general context – partially due to the shared pragmatic qualities of managerial responsibility and competence requirements (Nienaber & Roodt, 2008; Novicevic, Sloan, Duke, Holmes, & Breland, 2006; Wagner-Tsukamoto, 2007; Washbush, 2005; Wren, 2005). Leadership and management are identified as two distinct but inextricably interwoven functions (Kotter, 2001; Nienaber, 2010; Teleşpan & Halmaghi, 2012). Leadership inherently encompassed aspects of management, but management did not inversely incorporate all the leadership's functionalities (Armandi, Oppedisano, & Sherman, 2003; Kent, Crotts, & Azziz, 2001; Kotter, 2001; Pearce et al., 2003; Von Krosigk, 2007).

Management entailed responsibility for coordination, implementation, and accomplishment of daily organizational tasks, including the mitigation of complexities discovered from organizational changes through the use of the organization's resources and effective communication (Teleşpan & Halmaghi, 2012). Leadership involved the process of inspiring others with the ability to accomplish individual, group, or business goals and the execution of organizational change through the strategic decision-making based on the mission and vision (Atta-Panin, 2013; Dionne et al., 2013; Northouse, 2010; Yahaya et al., 2011).

Leadership was similar to entrepreneurship in terms of the individual. Leadership specifically focused on the individual's personality traits (Dubrin, 2013; Kumawat, 2009; Surie & Ashley, 2008). Leadership influenced others to accomplish a goal, whereas entrepreneurship emphasizes the individual's strategic-making process to exploit new opportunities (Murad, 2014; Renko, El Tarabishy, Carsrud, & Brännback, 2015). Entrepreneurial leadership incorporated the essential elements of leadership and entrepreneurship when combined.

Renko et al. (2015) define, "... entrepreneurial leadership as influencing and directing the performance of group members toward the achievement of organizational goals that involve recognizing and exploiting entrepreneurial opportunities" (p. 55). Entrepreneurial leadership concentrated on the prominence of the individual's process, attributes, and behavior toward realizing opportunity-focused activities. Entrepreneurial leadership theory adapted to transactional and transformational leadership styles.

Transactional and transformational leadership styles were introduced during the 20th century by Burns (1978) and Bass (1985). Transactional leadership was primarily based on job-performance rewards to accomplish objectives. Transactional leadership was influential and regularly interacted with subordinates for direct supervision of responsibilities to meet the targeted goals (Antonakis, Avolio, & Sivasurbramaniam, 2003; Bass & Avolio; 1993). The attributes of transactional leadership entailed the aspects outlined in the definition of management. An entrepreneur involved in a start-up or small business would need to utilize the transactional leadership style for daily operations.

In contrast, transformational leaders were visionary and enthusiastic, with a characteristic ability to inspire superior performance from subordinates (Bycio, Hackett, & Allen, 1995; Howell & Avolio, 1993). Transformational leadership focused on intellectually stimulating subordinates, which inspired creativity and innovation (Bass & Riggio, 2006). Transformational leadership was synonymous with attributes of entrepreneurial leadership. Entrepreneurial leadership involved recognizing and exploiting new opportunities, while transformational leadership inspired creativity and innovation.

A review of literature on leadership, not specifically centered on entrepreneurship, evolved through a series of independent theories. There are earlier leadership studies on traits, styles and behavior theory or situational and conditional theory. These theories were the foundation of present-day leadership research.

The pioneer of trait theory, Ralph M. Stogdill (1948), advocated that leadership's inherent characteristics were attributable to successful leaders. The personality and physical characteristics of the trait theory was the basis for the preliminary research in leadership. Stodgill's initial research identified the following listed traits as essential leadership qualities: physical, intelligence, knowledge, responsibility, integrity, emotional control, social skills, self-confidence, and responsibility.

The traits theory was useful during the industrial era as a measuring stick to evaluate the performance of leaders and developing the qualities of the leaders within the organization. However, the trait theory was difficult to validate and summarize in literature, exposing it to heavy criticism. Scholars argued the traits theory ignored the effect situations have on leadership and followers varies depended on their individual strengths and intensity of those traits. Researchers strived to find answers to the ambiguities in the trait's theory of leadership after much debate and focus turned to behavioral studies.

The style and behavior approach determined successful leaders adopted a democratic and participative methodology (Bowsers & Seashore, 1966). The style and behavior research had more categorization, which provided evidence to validate a viable leadership style. Neither the trait theory nor the style/behavior approach could account for situational factors in leadership. Leadership effectiveness seemed to contain complex variations.

Fiedler (1967) recognized these leadership intricacies and proposed a new perspective on task-oriented leadership, identified as a conditional theory of leadership. Situational and conditional theory determined the effectiveness of leadership relied on the leader's ability to diagnose the contributing factors, understand how the different factors can affect the leadership approach, and adjust the leadership approach based on the conditions (Ogbonna & Harris, 2000; Thamhain, 2005). The leader would adapt to the leadership style appropriate for the situation.

Education

A literature review of education in relation to entrepreneurship indicated a positive association with success (Tseng, 2013; Vij & Sharma, 2013; Zafar & Khan, 2014). In contrast, there was still debate over whether entrepreneurial skills could be taught. Hwang (2012) argued entrepreneurship is not clear-cut; therefore, real-world experience had to be acquired through 'doing' as opposed to a 'theory-based classroom setting.' Supposition would be that formal or informal education was a precursor to acquiring real-world experience to build on the business's functional competencies (e.g., human resources, finance, operations, and marketing), which circumvented the affiliated entrepreneurial pitfalls (Makhbul & Hasun, 2011). Entrepreneurship is a discipline that could be learned like any other discipline (Newbold & Erwin, 2014; Torrance, 2013; Wasserman, 2012).

In retrospection, scholars have noted the accountability for the random nature of entrepreneurship. A combination of rigorous academic education and exposure to activity-based practical applications of real-world situations would be an adequate approach to entrepreneurship's uncertain and unstructured environment (Izquierdo & Buelens, 2008; Radipere, 2012). Entrepreneurs could gain analytical skills through education to efficiently measure market needs of the recognized opportunity (Singh & Gibbs, 2013). There was evidence that education was an important vehicle for entrepreneurial enhancement and success: knowledge and skills, awareness, and independence (Raposo & do Paço, 2011; Sánchez, 2010).

The knowledge acquired through education stimulated the entrepreneurs' mentality toward unique ideas or solutions for needs in business expertise. Moreover, education could structure and define entrepreneurs' problem-solving, decision-making, strategic thinking, and networking skills (Putta, 2014). Education broadened the horizons of an entrepreneur's awareness of career alternatives and potential business opportunities. Greater visibility was gained on business potential that stretched the imagination for endless possibilities. Finally, education cultivated entrepreneurs' sense of autonomy and self-confidence. The entrepreneurs increased knowledge and skills, awareness, and independence will expand their minds creatively and innovatively (Raposo & do Paço, 2011).

According to Sonfield and Lussier (2014), entrepreneurs with a higher level of education had a significant correlation to a high degree of innovation with lower risk. This idea implied a greater degree of critical thinking used to reduce the risk associated with business ideas and solutions. Scholars and practitioners emphasized the theoretical learning concept for entrepreneurship androgogy was to concentrate on the ability to recognize and act on opportunities, as well as handle the ambiguities of newness centered on these opportunities (Pandey & Tewary, 2011; Zhao, Seibert, & Lumpkin, 2010).

Formal Education. Formal education was acquired through infrastructures that validated a level of proficiency. A formal education infrastructure could be an accredited college or certified training institution (Zafar & Khan, 2014). A majority of the research literature in reference to formal education for entrepreneurs focused on the tertiary or post-secondary educational level. "As an entrepreneur, the income returns to formal education were between 2-13% higher than as an employee" (van Praag, van Witteloostuijn, & van der Sluis, 2013, p. 392). Formal education was an environment fertilized with a wealth of knowledge and a playground for developing interpersonal skills and personal networks for an aspiring entrepreneur (Griffith, 2013).

Formal education provided entrepreneurs with a foundation of confidence, enhances human capital, and the aptitude to methodically process opportunities for potential business profits (Griffith, 2013). African-American entrepreneurs have the improved ability to remove barriers in business when equipped with a solid human capital foundation in formal education. Financial institutions used this (lack of education) barrier to exacerbate access to capital for African-American entrepreneurs (Arora, 2014; Biz Filings, 2012; Lofstrom & Bates, 2013; Small Business Notes, 2015).

African-American entrepreneurs involved in a business that provided professional services usually overcame the financial barrier(s). Professional service businesses often avoided the high-barrier business industry expense of large equipment and inventories (Lofstrom & Bates, 2013). The educational credentials required for most professional service businesses (e.g., Information Technology (IT), Program Management (PM), financial professionals) had a higher level of intellectual and human capital, which was considered a low-barrier industry. Low-barrier industries does not have the high demand of costly economy of scale, (i.e., business start-up, daily operation), expensive capital requirements (i.e., machinery, equipment), supplier/distribution, and regulatory hurdles unlike high-barrier industries. The collective value of intellectual and human capital (i.e., knowledge, business training, and proprietary information) gave entrepreneurs in the business of providing professional services a competitive advantage in the quest for financial capital (Lofstrom & Bates, 2013). Formal education was a societal measuring stick used by employers, financial institutions, and governments to quantify the level of proficiency in a particular profession. Degrees and accredited tests are required to obtain a license in specific professions (e.g., doctors, lawyers), and certifications are required for specialized occupations (e.g., Information Technology (IT), Program Management (PM)).

Informal Education. Informal education does not have organized accreditation or certification curriculums. Knowledge acquired from informal education can be sourced through conventional means of seminars, professional literature, the Internet, and other practical applications (i.e., scientific or didactic games, lectures, case studies, discussions) to update the knowledge base (Mwasalwiba, 2010; Rih & Guedira, 2014; Zafar & Khan, 2014). Entrepreneurs highly favored informal education as a quick source of knowledge acquisition. Empirical analysis indicated the majority of entrepreneurs (72%) used one-day seminars and reading professional literature as their preferable knowledge updating processes (Barbara, 2008, p. 170).

Informal education did not replace the attributed value of formal education, because formal education was a more tangible source to quantify the level of proficiency of entrepreneurs' human capital. Instead, informal education was a better platform for knowledge enhancement. Crnkic, Cizmic, & Sunje (2012) alluded that informal education empowered rapid knowledge acquisition to achieve a specific outcome in entrepreneurial activities. Consequently, the informal education curriculum must contain adaptive content to the entrepreneur's specific needs to generate creativity and innovation for the desired outcome effectively.

Summary

African Americans will inherently encounter challenges in the process of becoming successful entrepreneurs. The lack of access to capital, limited business experience, and entrepreneurial knowledge were associated byproducts from centuries of racial discrimination (National Association of Social Workers, 2015). African-American entrepreneurs could take action to alleviate the barriers of access to capital, leadership, business experience, and entrepreneurial knowledge by being proactive in the process of personal human capital development.

Leadership was intrinsically linked to entrepreneurship because both are centered on the individual. Leadership was specifically focused on the individual's personality traits (Dubrin, 2013; Kumawat, 2009; Surie & Ashley, 2008). Entrepreneurship emphasized the individual's strategic decision-making process to exploit new opportunities (Murad, 2014; Renko et al. 2015). Entrepreneurial leadership concentrated on the prominence of the individual's process, attributes, and behavior toward realizing opportunity-focused activities.

A significant amount of literature supported formal and informal education, along with experience, and contributed to the development of leaders (Alexander, 2013; Kinion, 2012; Lofstrom & Bates, 2013; Singh & Gibbs, 2013; Smith & Tang, 2013). The insight and abilities of a person transformed during an educational and experiential journey by learning to methodically process opportunities on a larger social-economical scale while cultivating entrepreneurial proficiency (Ivy, 2006; Sheppard, 2010).

CHAPTER THREE

METHODOLOGY

Restatement of the Purpose

This qualitative phenomenological study examined the lived experiences of how leadership experience and formal and informal education impacted the success of African-American entrepreneurs in Northern Virginia. The results added more depth to the body of existing literature. This research empowers nascent African-American entrepreneurs with formulas for success in leadership experience and formal and informal education.

This chapter discussed the research approach for this study, which is a qualitative phenomenological methodology. The content of the research methodology is as follows: research design, subjects, instrumentation, procedure, methodological assumptions, limitations, delimitations, data processing, and analysis.

Research Design

The research design utilized unstructured, open-ended questions administered through in-depth interviews to explore the participants' lived experiences. The researcher was the primary instrument for the interviews, data collection, data processing, and analysis. The independent variable for this study was entrepreneurship. The two dependent variables explored were leadership experience and education.

A qualitative approach supported the idea of utilizing the natural setting to explore the full spectrum of participants' experiences and behavior (Hennink, Hutter, & Bailey, 2010). The qualitative method was appropriate to explore the perception and insight of the participants' experiences and sought to understand and interpret the influences of behavior (Hennink et al., 2010). The advantage of qualitative analysis was the in-depth contextualized information captured from the participants' personal experiences (Lietz & Zayas, 2010). In comparison, the quantitative methodology had the limited capability to statistically test objective theories by examining the relationship between variables, which only produced numerical results (Creswell, 2009).

Phenomenological research was like a window that allowed the researcher to look into the consciousness of peoples' lived experiences. This opportunity was achieved through two phenomenological designs: hermeneutic and transcendental. The transcendental phenomenological design was the most capable inquiry to facilitate open dialogue, solicit information on lived experiences, and search for patterns and themes from participants for an in-depth understanding (Creswell, 2006; Moustakas, 1994; Neuman, 2011). The results from the data analysis produced "a combination of textual and structural descriptions to convey the overall essence of the experience" for a deeper understanding (Creswell, 2006, p. 60). The participants' personal experience was the central focus of a transcendental phenomenological design. In comparison, the hermeneutic phenomenological design was a reflective interpretation of the researcher derived from the historical antecedents or text about the phenomenon (Sloan & Bowe, 2014). The onus was on the researcher to identify the right experiences extracted from the historical antecedents, isolate the themes, and to develop a philosophical assumption in hermeneutic phenomenology.

The primary intent of this research was centered on two core questions that explored the factors surrounding the central phenomenon and presented the varied perspectives or meanings that participants held (Creswell 2012).

RQ1: What are the lived leadership experiences of successful African-American entrepreneurs providing professional, scientific, and technical services in Northern Virginia?

RQ2: What are the experiences of acquiring formal and informal education to successful African-American entrepreneurs providing professional, scientific, and technical services in Northern Virginia?

Subjects

This qualitative study involved the participation of 21 successful African-American entrepreneurs in

Northern Virginia as a sample of the population. According to the Survey of Business Owners (U. S. Census Bureau, 2007), there were a total of 2,103 African American businesses in Northern Virginia providing professional, scientific, and technical services (Code: 54) as identified by the North American Industry Classification System (NAICS). According to Hennink et al. (2010), qualitative research required a small number of participants to “gain a detailed understanding of a certain phenomenon, to identify socially constructed meanings of the phenomenon and the context in which a phenomenon occurs” (p. 84).

There was no definitive rule that identified the number of participants to use in a qualitative study. Baker & Edwards (2012) recommend a sample size between 12 to 20 participants for a qualitative methodology, considering the time allocation for the data gathering. Mason (2010) suggested that 20 and 30 participants were the most commonly used sample sizes based on the sample size and saturation in Ph.D. studies using qualitative interviews.

The technique used for this study was nonprobability sampling, which involved non-random volunteer sampling. According to Davis, Gallardo, and Lachlan (2012), the benefit of volunteer sampling was easier and potentially less expensive to administer than random sampling. Purposive sampling was used as the non-random sampling method because the predefined group identified as African Americans with the specific achievement of successful entrepreneurship as the sampling purpose (Lund Research, 2012).

A list of participants was assembled with evident demographics, experience, and expertise for the study. Therefore, the participant recruitment strategy was the snowball technique and networks (e.g., formal and informal). The snowball recruitment strategy involved asking the subject to refer other participants who meet the study criteria (Hennink et al., 2010). Recruitment through networks (e.g., ethical group associations, professional associations) was key to initially identifying participants (Hennink et al., 2010). The lists of prospective participants were extracted from the following: Fairfax County African-American Owned Business Statistics (Fairfax County Economic Development Authority, 2015), Nation's Most Successful Black-Owned Businesses (Black

Enterprise, 2014), Top Black Entrepreneurs of 2012 (Inc. 5000, 2013), and Top 25 Minority-owned Businesses in Virginia (Virginia Business, 2011).

The qualitative research method had the increased responsibility to ensure thoroughness and trustworthiness, so equally important were the participants selected for the study. The participants met the selection criteria and possessed the information explored to better understand the research topic. Thus, the qualitative approach was structured toward recognizing commonalities between types and categorizing the implications of these commonalities.

Instrumentation

The instrument used by the researcher was 13 unstructured, open-ended questions that guided each interviewee and took approximately 60-90 minutes, depending on the participants' articulated responses. The predetermined interview location was in the participants' natural setting(s), isolated from distractions. The participants were presented with the interview questions (Appendix C). The participants were also given a consent form (Appendix B) for an acknowledgment and signature before the interview.

Confidentiality. Confidentiality was accomplished through legal procedures, user's authentication data storage, and concealed identity. The consent form, approved by the Institutional Review Board (IRB), was provided to the participant for acknowledgment before the interview began.

Validity. The data consistency was validated by evaluating raw data, data reduction products, and process (Campbell, 1996). The purpose of validity was to ensure the questions were structured to measure the study's objectives. A qualitative methodology research expert reviewed the interview questions.

Reliability. The in-depth interviews were conducted with the participants and utilized digital audio recording supported by the confirmability method of hand-written notes. The answers to the open-ended interview questions, written comments, and recorded audio were analyzed after the interviews. The participants were consulted as part of the member-check procedure to review the results for creditability once the analysis was completed.

Trustworthiness. Trustworthiness was a rigorous scholarship that requires meticulously defined procedures to reduce the presence of research reactivity (Lietz, Langer, & Furman, 2006). Lietz and Zayas (2010) accentuated that research reactivity occurred when “the researcher or the study procedures exert an impact on the participants, thereby changing the findings of the study” (p. 191). Reactivity was an inescapable influence in a qualitative study because the researcher was a part of the interview process (Maxwell, 2013). The researcher engaged in reflexivity to manage the threats of reactivity and bias. Reflexivity involved actively building self-awareness of the influences that impacted participants. A written journal, audio recordings, and discussion with peers were reflective approaches to allow thoughtful consideration to understand how the researcher influenced the participants’ responses and affected the trustworthiness of the qualitative study (Lietz & Zayas, 2010; Maxwell, 2013). Trustworthiness was an umbrella term that encapsulated the criteria of credibility, transferability, dependability, confirmability, and authenticity. “Trustworthiness was established when the findings closely reflected the meanings as described by the participants" (Lietz et al., 2006, p. 444).

Procedures

The data collection procedure for this qualitative phenomenological study included the following: (a) building a list of participants, (b) scheduling interviews, (c) acquiring confidentiality agreement signatures, and (d) collecting data from the interviews.

The initial contact with potential participants used the formal and informal network recruitment strategy. Emails, phone calls, and office visits were used to provide information on the purpose of the research and solicit the subject's participation (Appendix A). The researcher built a list of participants, validated the research criteria with the participant's qualifications, discussed the interview's location and timeframe (i.e., duration, date, and time), explained voluntary and confidentiality, and introduced the snowball technique designed to recommend additional subjects who meet the research criteria.

Interviews were scheduled with the participants after receiving the Institutional Review Board's (IRB) approval. The participants received a formatted introduction, interview questions (Appendix C), and a consent form (Appendix B). The interview commenced after these documents were read and signed by the participants.

The data collection occurred in the natural setting of the participant with the intention of selecting an environment free from distractions. The instruments included the researcher, interview questions, note-taking material, and an audio recording device (Creswell, 2009). Professional transcribers processed the collected data (i.e., short notes, audio recordings, and clarity on interview answers). The professional transcriber services completed the Transcriber Confidentiality Agreement (Appendix D) to protect the sensitive information and participants' privacy.

Methodological Assumptions, Limitations, and Delimitations

Assumptions. The methodological assumptions were expectations of the researcher on the approaches used in qualitative research (Creswell, 2009). The assumption was the entrepreneurs were precise in the reflections of their entrepreneurship lived experiences. Another assumption was the digital recording device might have technical difficulties during the interview, and some rich information might be lost.

Limitations. The study population, location, and recruitment strategy had potential limitations (Hennink et al., 2010). The sample population was African-American entrepreneurs providing professional, scientific, and technical services (Code: 54) identified by the North American Industry Classification System (NAICS). The research location was restricted to Northern Virginia and Washington, DC. The limitations of the sample population and location potentially affected the number of subjects available to participate in the study. Therefore, the snowball technique (referrals) was used to overcome the challenge of finding subjects. The study was limited to these criteria due to the access of a larger population, and there was a high concentration of African-American entrepreneurs in the Northern Virginia area providing professional, scientific, and technical services.

Delimitations. The delimitations were the number of participants and the conditions imposed on the terms utilized in the study. There was a range of 12 to 20 subjects that met the participant's criteria of this qualitative study (Baker & Edwards, 2012). The number of participants was not representative of the population but was suitable for purposive sampling in developing an in-depth understanding (Hennink et al., 2010). Using 20-30 subjects for in-depth interviews was suitable for discovering 90-95% of the experiences if the participants provided an opulent description (Griffin & Hauser, 1993; Mason, 2010; Penner & McClement, 2008). Another delimitation was the business duration criteria of a minimum of five (5) years for a successful African-American entrepreneur.

Data Processing and Analysis

The data collection approach achieved the in-depth interviews. Four basic categories were used for data collection: interviews, observations, documents, and audiovisual materials (Jacob & Furgerson, 2012). Qualitative research was designed to collect as much detail as possible. Therefore, an open-ended inquiry was the best technique to capture the in-depth experiences of the participants. It was important to start the interview with simple questions to establish trust and connect with the interviewee before asking the more sensitive and controversial questions. Jacob and Furgerson (2012) suggested that, "six to ten well-written interview questions should be enough to keep the interview within an hour to an hour and a half" (p. 5). Short notes were taken to document the interviewee's responses. Audio equipment was utilized during the interview, so more attention could be focused on maintaining the connection with the interviewee (Jacob & Furgerson, 2012).

The data analysis approach was the gathering of qualitative data when utilizing the open-end inquiry technique to capture the in-depth experiences of participants. The bottom-up data analysis procedure was relevant to the adequacy of a prevailing phenomenon. The bottom-up approach was an inductive reasoning concept that functioned well in parallel with a phenomenological design study. Inductive reasoning started with investigating a specific phenomenon, analyzing the various data input to detect patterns and themes, and producing a theoretical conclusion (Research Methods Knowledge Base, 2006). The data process sequentially occurred as follows: transcribe the data, review the text data, consolidate and transcribe text data (follow-up interview for clarity), identify a pattern, and summarize the themes.

CHAPTER FOUR

RESULTS

Restatement of the Purpose

This qualitative phenomenological research aimed to examine the lived experiences of how leadership experience and acquisition of formal/informal education impacted the success of African-American entrepreneurs in Northern Virginia. The results added more depth to the body of existing literature and empower nascent African-American entrepreneurs with formulas for success in leadership experience and formal/informal education acquisition.

Organization and Presentation

The research was organized around the variables to gain a deeper understanding of the key to successful African-American entrepreneurs in experience and acquisition of knowledge. The 13 unstructured, open-ended interview questions were subsets to the research questions. The interview questions concentrated on entrepreneurship, experience (i.e., business, leadership/management), and knowledge acquisition (i.e., formal education, informal education).

Results

The results were organized by the demographics and the variables used for this study. The demographics presented a summary of the collective details of the participants for this study. The independent variable for this study was entrepreneurship. The two dependent variables were experience (i.e., business, leadership/management) and knowledge acquisition (i.e., formal education, informal education).

Demographics

Twenty-one successful African-American entrepreneurs participated in this dissertation research. All the participants were at the corporate level as the President or a Chief Executive Officer (CEO) with more than five years in successful business operations. The businesses provided professional, scientific, and technical services identified under the North American Industry Classification System (NAICS) as Code 54 in Northern Virginia, including Washington, DC. The name of the participants and businesses were removed from the study to protect privacy. Aliases represented each participant (e.g., Participant #1 - P1).

There were 46 potential participants contacted for this study using Network Recruitment Strategy (NRS) – 32 and Snowball Recruitment Strategy (SRS) – 14. The participation rate was 21 (54%), with 25 prospective participants (i.e., NRS – 19, SRS – 6) who declined, or positive contact could not be established. The NRS was initiated five months prior to conducting the interviews, contributing to the successful participation rate. The SRS was implemented during the interview process after receiving the referrals from the participants through the NRS.

The business ownership of the participants was either Incorporated (Inc.) - 81% or Limited Liability Corporation (LLC) - 19%. The number of participants who answered "yes" to entrepreneurial parents was 43% compared to the 76% of participants without entrepreneurial parents. The participants provide jobs for between 4-780 employees. The average annual gross receipts of the participants ranged from $800K to $65M. The average annual gross business receipts for female participants were $10.9M and for male participants was $25.6M per collected data. The gender distribution of the participants was females (43%) and males (57%), as shown in Table 1.

Table 1 - Gender Distribution

Gender	*N*	Percentage
Female	9	43
Male	12	57

The age ranges of the participants were between 32 to 75 years old, with the average age being 57 years old. The average age participants started in business is 41 years old was calculated from the collected data. The distributions of the ages are illustrated in **Error! Reference source not f ound.**.

Table 2 - Distribution of the Ages

Age Group	*N*	Percentage
30 - 39	1	5
40 - 49	4	19
50 - 59	8	38
60 - 69	5	24
70 - 79	3	14

The number of years in business ranged from six to 29 years, with an average of 16 years in business. Table 3 shows the distribution for the number of years in business.

Table 3 - Number of Years in Business

Years in Business	*N*	Percentage
5 to 10	5	24
11 to 15	7	33

Years in Business	*N*	Percentage
16 to 20	2	10
21 to 25	4	19
26 to 30	3	14

Entrepreneurship

It was important to identify with the participants from an entrepreneurial perspective while seeking deeper insight into their lived experiences. Therefore, four of the 13 interview questions were allocated to entrepreneurship. The entrepreneurship questions inquired about the motivation, challenges and obstacles, important entrepreneurial characteristics, and entrepreneurial advice of the participants.

Motivation. Question (Q) 1: Describe what motivated you to become an entrepreneur.

This question was designed to gain a more in-depth understanding of the factors surrounding the motivation for entrepreneurship. The question introduced the interview questions, which prepared the participants to tap into their mental recollection of the lived entrepreneurial experience. The emerging themes identified for motivation were illustrated in Table 4.

Table 4 - Motivation Emerging Themes

Motivation	*N*	Percentage
Opportunity-Advised-Inspired	8	23
Personal Satisfaction	7	20
Entrepreneurial Spirit	6	17
Professional Control	4	11
Income	3	9
Social Activism	3	9
Discrimination	2	6
Unemployment	2	6

The motivation factor with the larger number of eight (23%) responses was under the emerging theme of Opportunity-Advised-Inspired. Their influence came from family, professional associates, African-American entrepreneurs, or working in an environment that seamlessly presented the opportunity to transition into entrepreneurship. P5 stated, "We had a certain level of expertise, and there was a need for this expertise, so it appeared to be an easy marriage. We had the required expertise while working as a consultant supporting the company. We decided we were well-liked, and it was an easy transition to go from employee to an employer in forming my own company."

The next three emerging themes related heavily to the participants' desire for Personal Satisfaction - 7 (20%), Entrepreneurial Spirit - 6 (17%), and Professional Control - 4 (11%). In sequence with the emerging themes, the meaningful responses were as follows: P19 indicated, "I'd worked at several companies, and it's always been about the dollar. I wanted to ... disrupt what I call the management consulting industry by being more about the value than the dollar, so it was really in me to do better than what others in the area were doing"; "I think it's always been in me even as a kid"; and "to some degree independence."

Challenges and Obstacles. Q6: What challenges or obstacles did you encounter entering into business? How did you overcome these challenges or obstacles?

This question considered was more complex because the participants must recall difficult entrepreneurial experiences to include the strategy used to overcome these encounters. The emerging themes for challenges and obstacles are noted in Table 5.

Table 5 - Challenges and Obstacles Emerging Themes

Challenges and Obstacles	*N*	Percentage
Finance	16	31
Past Performance & Business Development	12	23
Discrimination	6	12
Employees	6	12
Professional Networks & Relationships	6	12
Client's Business Process	4	8
Mentorship	2	4

The challenges and obstacles interview question were strategically asked midway through the interview, after the participants were comfortable with the researcher, and they were provided detailed insight to the previously straightforward questions from the interview guide. Finance was the primary emerging theme with 16 (31%) shared experiences. The interview notes from P11 indicated he established a banking relationship with a community bank to overcome obstacles with finances.

The next emerging theme was Past Performance & Business Development, with 12 (23%) correlated responses. P1 emphasized:

> *Convincing agencies that you can still do the work even though you are small minority-owned. You got to do your homework; you need to know what you are talking about and know something about the agency (i.e., not knowing the mission of the agency, what problem they are experiencing), and even give them some stuff for free (e.g., white paper).*

Three other themes (e.g., discrimination, employees, and professional networks and relationships) generated the same amount of feedback of six participants (12%). The insight provided on the emerging theme of Discrimination is comparable to an omnidirectional antenna. The discriminatory experiences related various areas including finance, leasing agreements, and stereotypes (e.g., ethnicity, gender, age). P15 articulated a strategy to minimize the impact of discrimination: "I built a team that was a mixture ethnicities and backgrounds. It was a team concept with a diverse culture and the capability to perform, which allowed me to penetrate deeply into a clients' business culture; and rest is history." P2 echoed a similar message:

> *I had to hire a diverse set of employees to be strategic in obtaining new business. It's unfortunate the gender style in networking and obtaining business is the way it is now. Finance banks are still banks and there are too many objectives in the process and therefore discrimination is still into play. Well, we have a CFO for that and he looks different than me and it get me*

results. However, it is painful for me in understanding why this is still an issue in today's era.

Important Entrepreneurial Characteristics.

Q7: In your opinion, what are the most important entrepreneurial characteristics for business success?

The participants easily identified important entrepreneurial characteristics with detailed explanations. The preceding question of challenges and obstacles was used to identify important characteristics based on the participants' previous responses. The important entrepreneurial characteristics' emerging themes are in Table 6.

Table 6 - Important Entrepreneurial Characteristics Emerging Themes

Important Entrepreneurial Characteristics	*N*	Percentage
Tenacity	15	29
Planning	8	16
Integrity	6	12
Leadership	5	10

Important Entrepreneurial Characteristics	*N*	Percentage
Visionary	5	10
Financial Accountability	4	8
Humility & Humbleness	4	8
Knowledge & Skills	4	8

The key evolving theme for Important Entrepreneurial Characteristics is Tenacity, which was also identifiable by commitment, determination, fortitude, and persistence. There were 15 (29%) communal experiences associated with Tenacity. P10 voiced it best,

> *Determination would be the number one thing. There will be days that you will have to rethink and revise your ideals and know that there will be discouraging times and stay focused on it even when there is minimum support. Stay focused on your goal.*

Planning was the ensuing theme with eight participants (16%), and the follow-on emerging themes are equally important in identifying characteristics an aspiring entrepreneur must consider. The most powerful words were often disregarded as simplistic in stand-along terms. For example, P16, as an afterthought at the conclusion of the interview, stated, “find your humility!”

Entrepreneurial Advice. Q13: What advice would you have for others considering entrepreneurship?

A considerable amount of advice was provided by the participants on entrepreneurship. The most prominent entrepreneurial advice was summarized under the emergent theme of self-evaluation, and sequential emerging themes are expertise, resources, and innovation. Other experiences were difficult to categorize under a common emerging theme. Table 7 displays the emerging themes for entrepreneurial advice.

Table 7 - Entrepreneurial Advice Emerging Themes

Entrepreneurial Advice	*N*	Percentage
Self-evaluation	11	55
Expert of Your Craft	4	20

Entrepreneurial Advice	*N*	Percentage
Resources	3	15
Innovation	2	10

P17 verbalized straightforward and impactful entrepreneurial advice:

> *Never go in with the idea you know everything. In other words, this is all about being a sponge and make sure you're drinking clear water. Beware of the 3 Fs: Friends, Family, and Fools. You may have a good friend and decide you're going to start a business together and not put anything on paper. Do some documentation so that leverage of the relationship can't be used against you. Make sure they have the same vision, goals, and objectives and not try to use the relative (friendship) statute in your business. Family is a different matter, people have added family to the board of directors; from a legal*

> *standpoint, you should know what that means to your business. Fools, just stay away, plain and simple.*

P8's advice, in regards to leveraging resources, firmly recommended:

> *There are government programs out there, like the 8(a) Program. There is nothing the U.S. government has that we are not entitled to use. Especially if it is a legal program established by the Congress of the United States for the citizens of the United States. It belongs to you! You don't have to ask everybody for anything, you don't have to make excuses, you don't have to feel embarrassed. Go get it! Now, it is not a crutch. It should be a stepping stone.*

Experience

The term 'experience' was defined as business and leadership/management acumen for this study.

The purpose was to explore the business and leadership /management experience for greater insight from the participants. Thus, 5 of the 13 interview questions were assigned to the variable of experience. The experience questions queried the participants' leadership background, leadership development, prior business experience, gained business experience, and other relevant business experience.

Leadership Background. Q3: What was your leadership background entering into your current business?

The leadership background of the participants weighed heavily on experience from corporations and the military. A significant number of years contributed to the entrepreneurs developing leadership and management skills. Themes did surface to signify the vital roles of family and social activities. Table 8 exhibits the leadership background dynamics.

Table 8 - Leadership Background Emerging Themes

Leadership Background	*N*	Percentage
Corporate	13	41
Military	12	38
Social Activities	4	13
Family	2	6
Sports	1	3

The emerging theme of Corporate as a leadership background was commonly summarized by titles or positions, dollar amounts (paycheck), or the number of personnel supervised. The leadership background ancillary emergent theme of military consistently was framed by the years of military service caveated by the branch of service being periodically identified. It is important to note one participant does subscribe to more than one emerging theme.

Leadership Development. Q5: Describe how you developed your leadership to remain competitive in business.

There was always room for individual growth as a leader/manager of a small business. This question explored the entrepreneurs' lived experience in leadership and management development to remain competitive in their business industry. The emerging themes for the development of leadership experience were categorized in

Table 9.

Table 9 - Leadership Development Emerging Themes

Leadership Development	*N*	Percentage
Leadership Agility	15	38
Lessons Learned	13	33
Management	6	15
External Leadership Involvement	4	10
Leadership	2	5

Leadership Agility – 15 (38%) was the prevailing theme leading in the set of emerging themes for leadership development. Many of the participants came from a military background, which traditionally involved a more direct leadership style related to the culture. The participants from corporate America leadership style conformed to their level of authority and client base. The entrepreneurial environment required for the participants to adjust their previously learned leadership styles, so there was flexibility to adapt to the circumstances. P1 had to learn how to delegate for leadership agility as an entrepreneur, "I had a lot of learning and changing. I had to do learn how to delegate and trust others to do the job."

The next emergent theme for leadership development was Lesson Learned – 13 (33%), which included feedback and research. Leadership development meant to constantly evolve and to continually update your leadership's mental model. The client's mission, business regulation, and economy were always changing, so a lesson learned was imperative to appropriately develop leadership from business mistakes to remain competitive in business. P16 utilizes lessons learned as a normal practice for leadership development:

> *I feel like my leadership style has been developed through experience and mentors. I have a select group of advisors I could visit to continue my leadership development and learning*

from their experience of what went well and not so well. Now, when it doesn't go well, I learn and grow from it and learn what I do better the next time. We have management team meeting by placing everything on the table. From each perspective we can learn to examine what happened and how we learn do better moving forward collectively in the process. I think by addressing things head on it provides you with the necessary tools to move forward.

Prior Business Experience. Q2: Did you own any businesses prior to your current business? If so, how many years of business experience did you have prior to your current business?

The participants' response to prior business experience before the start of the currently successful business was "No" (70%) to the question. The remaining 30% of the participants responded with "Yes." The prior business experience is distributed equally between part-time and full-time basis. On a full-time basis, the prior business experience was in business between 2 - 13 years. The prior business experience on a part-time basis was in business between 1.5 - 2 years.

Gained Business Experience. Q4: Describe the business experience you had to achieve to remain competitive (in business).

The responses from the participants, on the gained business experiences, produced the emerging themes categorized by people, marketing, operations, and financial management. The emerging themes for accumulated business experience are in Table 10.

Table 10 - Gained Business Experiences Emerging Themes

Gained Business Experience	*N*	Percentage
People (Clients & Employees)	17	33
Marketing	12	23
Operations	10	19
Financial Management	7	13
Requirements	6	12

The most relevant phenomena of experience

shared by the participants was People – 17 (33%). The emergent theme of People incorporates gained business experience from clients, alliances (i.e., partnership, joint ventures, teaming), employees (i.e., hiring, managing, business relationships, communication, and building trust). P1 described gained business experience from the emerging theme of Peope:

> *Always try to look at head of the organization ... I would always watch how they handled themselves and what to do with people. They had different philosophies like different modes of operation but the one characteristic. I found they presented a personality of our confidence, direction, and demonstrated an ability to motivate people either through fear or through ... one guy was get the job done or I'm going to fire you. I found the other guy was, 'let's work together and make sure we all communicate to make this thing happen.' Another guy was, 'I put this*

> *thing together and I hire good people and I expect you to do the job and let me know when you need help.' So, I kind of used all those philosophies to mold me into what I am today.*

The second theme to materialize was Marketing – 12 (23%), which included networking, briefings, and presentations. P12 gained business experience manifested through joining advisory boards and councils for networking, information, and people. The third emergent theme was Operations – 10 (19%), defined as business operations and business certifications. P16's gained business experience was from business certifications acquired for a strategic advantage,

> *We strategically acquired Historically Underutilized Business Zones (HUBZone), Small Business Administration (SBA), and the 8(a) Business Development Program; we have the International Organization for Standardization (ISO 9000) quality*

management certifications; and are pursuing a Capability Maturity Model Integration (CMMI) level certification.

Other Relevant Business Experience. Q12: Would you share any other business experiences relevant to this study?

This question recognizes other relevant experiences considered for this study or be outlined for future research on successful African-American entrepreneurs. The emerging themes for different relevant business experiences are in Table 11.

Table 11 - Other Relevant Business Experiences Emerging Themes

Other Relevant Business Experience	*N*	Percentage
Spirituality	5	22
Communication Skills	4	17
Support Infrastructure	4	17
Ethics	4	17
Self-awareness	3	13
Social Entrepreneurship	3	13

The highest-ranking emergent theme materialized from the participant interviews was Spirituality – 5 (22%). The pitch and tone of the participants' voices carried a special emphasis when describing Spirituality. The transcribed words from the interviews do not convey the emotion (e.g., pitch and tone of voice) that conveyed the participants' empathy in relating their opinions of the importance of religion, their expressed connection with a spiritual entity, and the reliance upon their faith. P10's foundation of relevancy was driven by spirituality "Have faith! It was key for me. Everybody may not be into the religious aspect. For me it was key; for me, the divine direction." Rotter (1966) reveals the spirituality of an entrepreneur as an external locus of control, which simply means the entrepreneur believes destiny is controlled by external forces (e.g., fate, God, other power forces).

Conversely, the other type of locus of control is internally and the entrepreneur believes they have influence over the outcome in the life. An entrepreneur with an internal locus of control tends to be more self-reliant and independent (Shapero, 1975; Pandey & Tewary, 2011)."

The subsequent emerging themes were Communication Skills, Support Infrastructure, and Ethics. All were equal in the number of participants' collective experience – 4 (17%). "Surround yourself with very positive, like-minded people, and when you think you can't go any further, you keep going!" as captured in the interview notes from P16. P4 ethical enforcement ensured, "Your managers are loyal and trustworthy." P8's adage for support infrastructure was:

> *You want to employ a person who has strength, management skills, and knowledge of the business. You don't want to choose him in terms of friendship or relationship. You want to make sure that those bottom qualities are there and are solid before we go to the next level.*

Education

The education variable had two subcategories: formal and informal education. The intent was to understand what type of education was acquired and how instrumental education had been for the participants. Therefore, four of the 13 interview questions were assigned to education. The education questions investigate the level of formal education, benefits of formal education, level of informal education, and advantages of the participants' informal education.

Formal Education. Q8: Describe the formal education you had to acquire to sustain your business.

When the responses were compared during data analysis, the formal education- isolated themes displayed the following results: Only 33% of the participants actively acquired additional formal education. In comparison, 67% of the participants did not acquire formal education after starting their current business. The distribution of formal education acquired to sustain the business is presented in Table 12.

Table 12 - Distribution of Formal Education (Sustainment of Business)

Formal Education	*N*	Percentage
None	12	57
Certifications	6	29
Associates	1	5
Masters	1	5
Doctorates	1	5

The most significant emergent theme was personal certifications – six (29%), aside from participants obtaining no formal education after starting the current business. The Project Management Professional certification was acknowledged by three of the participants.

It was critically important to build traceability between the formal education acquired before and after the start of their business from a holistic perspective. Figure 2 illustrated the distribution of formal education acquired before starting the participants' current business as captured from the demographics section in the interview guide.

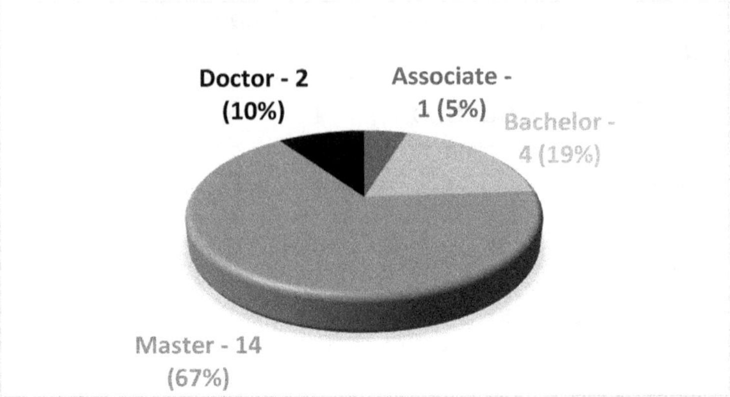

Figure 2 - Distribution of Formal Education (Before Starting Business)

Formal Education Benefits. Q9: How was formal education instrumental to your business success? The benefits of formal education for business success are displayed in Table 13.

Table 13 - Benefits of Formal Education (Sustainment of Business)

Formal Education Benefits	*N*	Percentage
Decision-making & Opportunity Recognition	7	39
Confidence	3	17
Finance	3	17
Increased Business Prospects	3	17
Accomplishment	2	11

Decision-making and opportunity recognition was the higher ratio emergent theme noted for benefits received from formal education. P7 stated the following in reference to the benefits of formal education:

> *The Project Management Professional (PMP) certification taught me that everything we do in life really is a project … it shows me that you can make a project out of those smallest things, which translate over into the workplace in how effective you get things done. It taught me efficiency; it taught me how to ensure the completion of a task with regard to conflict, and stabilization reconstruction really is how to manage conflict. Not every conflict gets solved but having it come to a happy medium compromise. Sometimes it takes a long time to solve issues. How to manage conflict, but also how to compromise, as well as the steps to compromise and*

conflict destabilization or conflict stabilization that's related to the workplace everything. With regard to Defense Acquisition University/ Defense Acquisition Workforce Improvement Act *(DAU/DAWIA), which is the U.S. Government's certification process for the acquisition, technology, and logistics career field. It essentially showed me the rigidity of contracts and the acquisition process and the fundamentals in which the people on the other side operated are coming from - so I can understand where they are coming from, as opposed to, they may not understand where I'm coming from, as a vendor. Yes, the government, yes. So it has helped me in the way that it has helped me not only understand where they are coming from but also how to toe the line on acquisition procedures and processes and actually know where the line is correct.*

Confidence, finance, and increased business prospects were the next ranked emerging themes of the benefits of formal education. These themes were noted in three (17%) of each participant's correspondence. P3 specified, "It is certification as an individual, as well as at the corporate level. What certifications have done is set us apart from our competition."

Informal Education. Q10: Describe the informal education you had to acquire to sustain your business. The distribution of informal education acquired to sustain the business is noted in Table 14.

Table 14 - Distribution of Informal Education (Sustainment of Business)

Informal Education Benefits	*N*	Percentage
Training	15	33
People & Organizations	15	33
Research & Reading	9	20
Programs	3	7
Audio	2	4

Informal Education Benefits	*N*	Percentage
Family Business	1	2

The two competing emerging themes were as follows: 1) training and 2) people and organization. They both accumulating 15 (33%) advocated experiences from the participants. Training was defined as an event that was short in duration (e.g., 1 to 5 days) such as a seminar, webinar, workshop, or conference. In contrast, a program was defined as an event long in duration with multiple iterations, without an accredited proficiency level test upon completion. The people and organization emerging theme was defined as people (i.e., other business owners, mentors, networks) and organizations (i.e., Small Business Administration (SBA), Veteran Outreach Business Center (VBOC), Procurement Technical Assistance Program (PTAP), Service Corps of Retired Executives (SCORE), and other formalized entities).

The third emerging theme of research and reading – nine (20%) was depicted as participants' informal education method for rapid knowledge acquisition. P21 reflections regarding reading were noted after the conclusion of the interview session. P21 emphasized “read something 15 minutes a day on a subject you want to be knowledgeable in, and you will be an expert in the year.”

Informal Education Benefits. Q11: How was informal education instrumental to your business success? The benefits of informal education for business success are listed in Table 15.

Table 15 - Benefits of Informal Education (Sustainment of Business)

Informal Education Benefits	*N*	Percentage
Information & Knowledge Acquisition	13	76
Business Opportunities	2	12
Establishing Business Relationship	1	6
Skills	1	6

Information and knowledge acquisition – 13 (76%) for informal education was the predominant emergent theme. The involvement in informal education was significantly higher than in formal education after the participants started the business. This result aligns with the findings discovered in the literature review on informal education. According to an empirical analysis by Barbara (2008), a majority of entrepreneurs (72%) preferred informal education for knowledge acquisition. P13's reflective insight on informal education resonated in the mindset of most of the participants and previous research on informal education:

> *I think that was even more instrumental than formal education because it's the real world; you're seeking out someone who has done it and someone who may be experiencing the same challenges or hurdles or phases of business growth that you will have to endure.*

Summary

The variables used for this study were entrepreneurship, experience (i.e., business, leadership, management), and education (i.e., formal, informal). The independent variable was entrepreneurship, and the dependent variables were experience and education. The research questions are formed from these variables and are as follows:

Research Question 1 (RQ1): What are the lived leadership experiences of successful African-American entrepreneurs providing professional, scientific, and technical services in Northern Virginia?

Research Question 2 (RQ2): What are the experiences of acquiring formal/informal education in relation to successful African-American entrepreneurs providing professional, scientific, and technical services in Northern Virginia?

The 13 unstructured, open-ended interview questions were categorized by the research questions to include the independent variable of entrepreneurship, as demonstrated in Chapter 4. The findings were based on the emerging themes identified from the analyzed results. There was multiple emerging theme discovered in the qualitative phenomenological study.

Table 16 exemplifies the leading emerging

themes for the categories of entrepreneurship, experience, and education.

Table 16 - Leading Emerging Themes

Variables	Core Themes	Leading Emerging Themes
Entrepreneurship	Motivation	1) Opportunity-Advised-Inspired; 2) Personal Satisfaction
	Challenges and Obstacles	1) Finance; 2) Past Performance & Business Development
	Important Entrepreneurial Characteristics	1) Tenacity; 2) Planning
	Entrepreneurial Advice	1) Self-evaluation; 2) Expert of your Craft
Experience	Leadership Background	1) Corporate; 2) Military
	Leadership Development	1) Leadership Agility; 2) Lesson Learned
	Prior Business Experience	30 % owned a business previously
	Gained Business Experience	1) People; 2) Marketing
	Other Relevant Business Experience	1) Spirituality; 2) Communication Skills, Support Infrastructure, & Ethics
Education	Formal Education	1) None; 2) Certifications

	Formal Education Benefits	1) Decision-making & Opportunity Recognition; 2) Confidence, Finance, & Increased Business Prospects
	Informal Education	1) Training; 2) People & Organizations
	Informal Education Benefits	1) Information & Knowledge Acquisition; 2) Business Opportunities

CHAPTER FIVE

DISCUSSION, CONCLUSIONS, AND RECOMMENDATIONS

Discussion

This qualitative phenomenological study aimed to examine the lived experiences of how leadership experience and acquisition of formal/informal education impact the success of African-American entrepreneurs in Northern Virginia. The written descriptions were analyzed to sequester the emerging themes and gave voice to the experiences charted in the study.

Academic literature provided reasons why African-American entrepreneurs failed in business. Minimal research evidence existed on successful African-American entrepreneurs' proven business characteristics, traits, and practices. There are African Americans who have established successful businesses despite centuries of discrimination that led to the social impacts of access to capital, limited business experience, and entrepreneurial knowledge (DeCaro et al., 2010; Kinion, 2012; Lofstrom & Bates, 2013; Robinson, 2014; Singh, & Gibbs, 2013; Smith & Tang, 2013).

The sample population for this qualitative study included 21 successful African-American entrepreneurs in Northern Virginia, including Washington, DC. The interviews of these successful African-American entrepreneurs involved exploring the meaning of their lived experience in relation to business, leadership/management, and the acquisition of education.

Conclusions

A majority of the participants (95%) were extremely interested in sharing their entrepreneurial experiences after learning the study's details. Participant (P4) normally avoided involvement in research and studies but elected to participate since the interview time was already on the calendar. Afterward, P4 found the interview beneficial because it allowed an opportunity to think about aspects of themselves and their business not seriously considered before the interview.

Two participants (P9 and P11) declined the audio recording for the interview, and the mitigation strategy was to ensure the interview notes captured the detailed essence of their valuable experiences. Two participants (P8 and P9) insisted on reviewing the interview questions prior to their approval of participation. The researcher did inquire as to why these participants needed to review the interview questions to determine their participation. The participants' business operation supported a niche market and desired to avoid discussion in reference to their internal operations. The mitigation strategy minimized bias and reactivity of interview questions prior to the actual interview via a careful evaluation of the articulated responses during the researcher's reflectivity. The bias and reactivity were minimal compared to these participants' rich and valuable insight.

According to Maxwell (2013), reactivity was virtually an inescapable influence due to the researcher's involvement in qualitative studies during the interview process. The researcher engaged in reflexivity to manage the threats of reactivity and bias. Reflexivity involved actively building self-awareness of the influences that impact participants.

Entrepreneurship

The emerging themes for motivation correlated with findings exposed in the literature review. The African-American entrepreneur's transition from employee status was motivated by the disparities within the workforce, the desire to gain more control over job satisfaction, career advancements, and economic independence, as well as to have a viable option compared to unemployment (Alexander, 2013; Griffith, 2013). P3's lived experience was sincerely straightforward: "Basically, gotten to what I perceived to be a glass ceiling harder than glass, but I had kind of gone as far as I could go working for someone else." Conversely, Opportunity-Advised-Inspired was the emergent theme with the most occurrences under the core theme of Motivation. The emergent theme of Opportunity-Advised-Inspired was summarized by the experiences that motivated the participants to become entrepreneurs. The participants recalled these occurrences as if they transpired yesterday. The most frequently noted detail was how the successful African-American entrepreneurs were inspired or advised by other African-American entrepreneurs. It was hard to translate the passion in the participants' voices during the reflection of these experiences. These moments elicited a surge of 'can do' energy with a rite of passage to progress toward entrepreneurship. It was hard not to be inspired by these stories.

Unfortunately, entrepreneurial experiences of inequalities were discovered in the challenges and obstacles emergent theme. The entrepreneurs did introduce strategies to overcome these inequalities. The entrepreneurial advice from the emerging themes carried a concentrated focus centered on self-evaluation and being an expert in the craft. Some emerging themes were unable to be established as a correlated pattern for a few experiences shared by the participants. Nevertheless, the importance of each shared advice and experience still provided rich and valuable insight for nascent (budding) entrepreneurs.

Experience

All the participants had a strong leadership background, which served as a foundation to guide their entrepreneurial endeavors. Corporate and Military experience were the two primary emerging themes for leadership background. The participants honed their leadership by serving in roles and positions that impacted their organizations (in both leadership cases). The participants were accustomed to working in positions outside of the norm and performing above and beyond the requirements of their leadership roles. Their leadership background included vice presidents, directors, chairpersons of boards, program managers, and leadership positions. Early in the interview process, it became apparent self-confidence and high ambitions were related to the desire to serve in prominent leadership roles along their career path.

Although participants had minimal prior experience operating an entire business entity based on the data collected from the core theme of prior business experience, the participants' leadership background in various leadership roles was enough for a successful transition to entrepreneurship. Their eagerness to succeed in business and enthusiasm to learn and grow empowered their leadership development and the ability to gain business experience to remain competitive in business. The keynote to encapsulating the emerging themes for leadership development and gained business experience was business success did not come from operating in a vacuum. Socialization and evaluation (e.g., self and business) were key factors to succeeding in business. Socialization meant networking, partnership, mentorship, and knowing how to interact with people (e.g., employees and clients). Evaluation meant capitalizing on lessons learned, being open to feedback and new ideas, performing Strength, Weakness, Opportunity & Threat (SWOT), root-cause, and other process improvement analysis tools/techniques. The business world's needs and demands were forever changing, which meant entrepreneurs had to constantly grow and change with the needs and demands of the business world.

Education

All the participants achieved some level of formal education (e.g., a college degree) prior to starting a business. The participants level of formal education was graduate (Master's) degree – 14 (67%) based on the collected demographic data. It was reasonable to suggest the high level of formal education was due to the industry the participants operated within, which were professional, scientific, and technical services.

After the participants started in business, the emergent theme for formal education shifted significantly to certifications. The certifications attained while in business are specific to their industry's professional and technical services, which are Project Management Professional (PMP), Information Technology (IT), and other accreditations obtained through the U.S. government and civilian organizations to validate a level of proficiency. The primary benefits of the attained formal education were decision-making and opportunity recognition. The formal education gave participants the credibility, confidence, and knowledge to identify opportunities and make decisions on pursuing business prospects.

Informal education was the preferred method for knowledge acquisition. The emerging themes of people and organizations, research and reading, and training were the most utilized means to acquire specific knowledge. The people and organization and research and reading emergent themes appeared to be interwoven with aspects of the experience core theme, linked to the discussion of socialization and evaluations. The organization portion involved the participants using Small Business Administration (SBA), Veteran Outreach Business Center (VBOC), Procurement Technical Assistance Program (PTAP), Service Corps of Retired Executives (SCORE), and other similar resources.

The overarching benefit from informal education that materialized was information and knowledge acquisition. The key to the participants' business success in relation to informal education was acquiring information rapidly for pending business decisions. The ability to search the Internet, consult with fellow entrepreneurs who have successfully navigated specific business situations, or tap into an organization for additional business or industry information were all quintessential elements of knowledge acquisition through informal education.

There were instances where the participants used an information education program for strategic planning of the business direction or new ideas for business growth. The emergent theme of programs captured the participants' experience with thinking long-term on larger scales to grow the business by attending programs such as Goldman Sachs 10,000 Small Businesses Program, Tuck Executive Program, and Harvard Executive/Cohort Program.

Implications for Practice

Unlimited research literature was available on identified problems for African-American entrepreneurs, but limited research existed relative to qualitative solutions to these problems, as stated earlier in this study. This qualitative study added more depth to the body of existing literature. This new knowledge empowered nascent African-American entrepreneurs with formulas for success in the areas of experience (e.g., business, leadership/management) and acquisition of knowledge (e.g., formal and informal education).

The identified emerging themes were generated from experiences shared by African-American entrepreneurs who overcame problems novice entrepreneurs would eventually face in business. The unstructured entrepreneurship environment was not clear-cut and had a high level of uncertainty. It would be most beneficial to review the strategies and solutions voiced in this research to avoid pitfalls and shortcomings from not being prepared to triumph over the ambiguities in entrepreneurship. These participants' valuable advice can serve as an entrepreneurial pedagogy resource to assess business ambiguities, formulate strategies, and convert the uncertainty into a business opportunity (Pandey & Tewary, 2011; Zhao et al., 2010).

In addition, it was advantageous for entrepreneurs to conduct a thorough self-evaluation to measure the entrepreneurial aspects within their control (i.e., business, leadership/management, and education) and survey the business industry's landscape. Novice African-American entrepreneurs were highly recommended for research organizations that specialized in assisting with starting a business (e.g., Economic Development Authority, Small Business Administration). Nascent African-American entrepreneurs are encouraged to develop an affiliation with establishments or groups to promote entrepreneurial education to include a nurturing atmosphere for networking. Finally, use the findings from this research and your self-evaluation to implement a Strength, Weakness, Opportunity & Threat (SWOT) analysis, preferably with a seasoned entrepreneur from the business industry of interest.

Recommendations for Further Research

The recommendations for future research were to implement mixed-method research, change the geographical location and industry, utilize different research variables, and explore the entrepreneurial development of children in the area of technology and globalization. Mixed-method research took advantage of the qualitative and quantitative research strengths while reducing the inherent limitations of each research method (Truscott et al., 2010). Therefore, mixed-method research on executable solutions to the problems African-American entrepreneurs experience in business strengthened the findings of the existing body of literature.

Future research was recommended targeting successful African-American entrepreneurs using a different geographical location and industry. The geographical limitations of this study were limited to the location of Northern Virginia and Washington, D.C. The industry used for this study was limited to the North American Industry Classification System (NAICS) code 54, known as professional, scientific, and technical services. A higher level of formal education and professional skill-intensive expertise was a prerequisite for black-owned businesses in Northern Virginia providing services in this industry. Additional research in other geographical locations and industries would be advantageous in expanding the scope and identify more detailed solutions for African-American entrepreneurs.

A recommendation for continually materialized solutions for African-American entrepreneurs would require future research using additional variables identified in this study. The results from the emerging themes unveiled a variety of aspects outside the boundaries of the framed variables used in this study. These themes presented some ancillary value to the overall study. A deeper understanding of the best solutions or approaches for African-American entrepreneurs in the following areas would increase the entrepreneurial knowledge bandwidth: mentor/protégé relationship, business networking and communication skills, social entrepreneurship, and financial strategies.

African Americans are at an inherent disadvantage entering into entrepreneurship due to the lack of historical family business experience, entrepreneur support infrastructure, or network systems to recognize, analyze, and cultivate business opportunities (Fairlie & Robb, 2008). For these reasons, future research was recommended on establishing an efficient and productive mentor/protégé relationship with nascent African-American entrepreneurs. An accurate assessment of nascent African-American entrepreneur's business knowledge was critical in the earlier stages of a mentor/protégé relationship. The business knowledge assessment identified the entrepreneur's strengths and weaknesses, so the mentor and protégé began the relationship at a level that accounted for gaps and areas of weakness in business.

A recommendation for future research utilizing the variables of social entrepreneurship, networking, and business communication skills would be beneficial to novice African-American entrepreneurs to establish a support infrastructure and network system. The inability to strategically plan and control financial capital were pronounced reasons for African American entrepreneurs' business failure (Brown, 2014). Therefore, research was recommended to explore financial strategies for African-American entrepreneurs before and during their business ventures. Additional financial strategies research could increase African-American, entrepreneurs' business astuteness on financial and lending institutions' business loan qualifications and practices.

There were continued conversations with a majority of the participants after the conclusion of the interviews. A reoccurring discussion was in reference to their children's entrepreneurial development, which was traceable to the demographic question, "Were your parents entrepreneurs?"

The researcher found it interesting to discover a majority of the adult children of the participants either worked for the family business or started their own business. The participants exposed and involved their children in business at an early age. It would be beneficial to conduct future research on 21st century African-American entrepreneurs to understand proven methods used to prepare their children for entrepreneurship in the era of technology and globalization.

REFERENCES

Ahn, T. (2011). Racial differences in self-employment exits. *Small Business Economics, 36*, 169–186. doi: 10.1007/s11187-009-9209-3

Alexander, N. H. (2013). *A phenomenological exploration of self-directed learning among successful minority entrepreneurs.* Retrieved from ProQuest Dissertation Publishing. (UMI 3567829).

Antonakis, J., Avolio, B. J., & Sivasurbramaniam, N. (2003). Context and leadership: An examination of the nine-factor, full-range leadership theory using the multifactor leadership questionnaire. *The Leadership Quarterly*, *14*(3), 261-295.

Armandi, B., Oppedisano, J., & Sherman, H. (2003). Leadership theory and practice: A case in point. *Management Decision, 41*(10), 1076-1088.

Arora, R. (2014). *What you need for a small business loan.* Retrieved from http://smallbusiness.foxbusiness.com/finance-accounting/2014/06/05/what-need-for-small-business-loan/

Atta-Panin, J. (2013). Leadership and strategic management. *GSTF International Journal on Business Review, 3*(1), 14-22. doi: 10.5176/2010-4804_3.1.283

Badenhausen, K. (2013). *Virginia tops 2013 list of the best states for business.* Retrieved from http://www.forbes.com/sites/kurtbadenhausen/2013/09/25/virginia-tops-2013-list-of-the-best-states-for-business/

Bagheri, A., & Pihie, Z. A. (2011). Entrepreneurial leadership: Towards a model for learning and development. *Human Resource Development International, 14*(4), 447–463.

Baker, S. E., & Edwards, R. (2012). How many qualitative interviews is enough? *National Centre for Research Methods Review Paper, 1*, 1-42.

Banks, J. A. (2012). *Encyclopedia of Diversity in Education* (Vol. 1). Thousand Oaks, CA: Sage Publication Inc.

Baskerville, R. F. (2003). Hofstede never studied culture.

Accounting, Organizations and Society, 28(1), 1-14.

Bass, B. M. (1985). *Leadership and performance beyond expectations*. New York, NY: Free Press.

Bass, B. M., & Avolio, B. J. (1993). Transformational leadership and organizational culture, *Public Administration Quarterly, 17*(1), 112–17.

Bass, B. M., & Riggio, R. E. (2006). *Transformational leadership*. Mahwah, NJ: Lawrence Erlbaum Associates, Inc.

Bennett, J., Fry, R., & Kochhar, R. (2020). *Are you in the American middle class?* Pew Research Center. Retrieved from https://www.pewresearch.org/fact-tank/2020/07/23/are-you-in-the-american-middle-class/

Benton, L. (2012). *Racial inequality in modern day America*. Retrieved from http://www.srwolf.com/wolfsoc/soc204/204archives/2012/12/13/racial_inequality_in_modern_da.php

Biz Filings. (2012). *What banks look for when reviewing loan applications*. Retrieved from http://www.bizfilings.com/toolkit/sbg/finance/getting-financing/what-banks-look-for-reviewing-loan-applications.aspx

Black Enterprise. (2014). *BE 100s: The nation's largest Black-owned business*. Retrieved from http://www.blackenterprise.com/lists/be-100s-2014/

Blanchflower, D., Levine, P., & Zimmerman, D. (2003). Discrimination in the small business credit market. *Review of Economics and Statistics, 85*(4), 930–943.

Bogan, V., & Darity W. (2008). Culture and entrepreneurship? African American and immigrant self-employment in the United States. *The Journal of Socio-Economics, 37*, 2000-2019.

Bone Research (2014). *Minority entrepreneurs face discrimination when seeking loans.* Retrieved from http://search.proquest.com/docview/1532672063?accountid=34899

Bontas, D. (2012). Management and leadership in business. *Economy Transdisciplinarity Cognition, 15*, 83-92.

Bosma, N., Wennekers, S., & Amorós, J. E. (2011). *Global Entrepreneurship Monitor 2011 Global Report*. Babson College, Babson Park, MA.

Bowsers, D. G., & Seashore, S. E. (1966). Predicting organizational effectiveness with a four-factor theory of leadership. *Administrative Science Quarterly, 11*, 238–63.

Brown, C., & Thornton, M. (2013). How entrepreneurship theory created economics. *Quarterly Journal of Austrian Economics, 16*(4), 401-419.

Brown, C. M. (2014). *5 reasons why small business fail.* Retrieved from http://www.blackenterprise.com/small-business/5-reasons-why-small-businesses-fail/

Brown, E. S. (2014). *The professional Black class: Race, class, and community in the post-civil rights era.* New York, NY: Routledge.

Burns, J. M. (1978). *Leadership*. New York, NY: Harper & Row.

Bycio, P., Hackett, R. D., & Allen, J. S. (1995). Conceptualization of transactional and transformational leadership. *Journal of Applied Psychology*, *80*(4), 468–78.

Campbell, T. (1996). Technology, multimedia, and qualitative research in education.

Journal of Research on Computing in Education, *30*(9), 122-133.

Carter, J. L. (2014). *For Black America, the only jobs that await are jobs HBCUS help to create.* Retrieved from http://www.huffingtonpost.com/jarrett-l-carter/for-black-america-only-jobs_b_5366657.html

Cavalluzzo, K., & Wolken, J. (2005). Small business loan turndowns, personal wealth and discrimination. *Journal of Business, 78*, 2153–2178.

Coarse, R. H. (1937). The nature of the firm. *Economica, 4*(16), 386-405.

Cooper, A. C., & Dunkelberg, W. C. (1987). Entrepreneurial research: Old questions, new answers, and methodological issues. *American Journal of Small Business, 3*, 11-23.

Commonwealth of Virginia. (2015). *Northern Virginia: Description*. Retrieved from http://www.virginia.org/regions/NorthernVirginia/

Covin, J. G., & Slevin, D. P. (1991). A conceptual model of entrepreneurship as firm behavior. *Entrepreneurship theory and practice*, *16*(1), 7-25.

Creswell, J. W. (2006). *Qualitative inquiry and research design: Choosing among five approaches* (2nd ed.). Thousand Oaks, CA: SAGE Publication.

Creswell, J. W. (2009). *Research design: Qualitative, quantitative, and mixed methods approaches* (3rd ed.). Thousand Oaks, CA: SAGE Publications.

Creswell, J. W. (2012). *Research design: Qualitative, quantitative, and mixed methods approaches* (3rd ed.). Thousand Oaks, CA: SAGE Publication.

Crnkic, K., Cizmic, E., & Sunje, A. (2012). *Knowledge management and innovation as driving forces behind successful entrepreneurship*. 6th International Conference of the School of Economics and Business, University of Sarajevo, School of Economics and Business, Bosnia and Herzegovina.

Cuervo, A., Ribeiro, D., & Roig, S. (2007). *Entrepreneurship: Concepts, theory and perspective*. New York, NY: Springer.

Danes, S. M., Lee, J., Stafford, K., & Heck, R. K. Z. (2008). The effects of ethnicity, families and culture on entrepreneurial experience: An extension of sustainable family business theory. *Journal of Developmental Entrepreneurship, 13*(3), 229–268.

Davidson, M. J., Fielden, S. L., & Omar, A. (2010). Black, Asian and minority ethnic female business owners: Discrimination and social support. *International Journal of Entrepreneurial Behaviour & Research, 16*(1), 58-80.

Davis, C. S., Gallardo, H. P., & Lachlan, K. (2012). *Straight talk about communication research methods* (2nd ed.). Dubuque, IA: Kendall-Hunt Publishing.

DeCaro, F. P., DeCaro, N., & Bowen-Thompson, F. O. (2010). An examination of leadership styles of minority business entrepreneurs: A case study of public contracts. *Journal of Business & Economic Studies, 16*(2), 72-79.

Department of the Army. (2010). *Field Manual (FM) 5-0: The operations process*. Retrieved from https://fas.org/irp/doddir/army/fm5-0.pdf

Dionne, S. D., Gupta, A., Sotak, K. L., Hao, K. C., Kim, D. H., & Yammarino, F. J. (2013). A 25-year perspective on levels of analysis in leadership research. *The Leadership Quarterly, 25*(1), 6-35.

Dubrin, A. J. (2013). *Leadership: Research findings, practices, and skills* (7th ed.). Mason, OH: Cengage Learning. Retrieved from http://www.cengagebrain.com.au/content/9781133926382.pdf

Equal Justice Initiative. (2014). *A history of racial injustice*. Retrieved from http://racialinjustice.eji.org/timeline/1610s/

Fairfax County Economic Development Authority. (2015). *Fairfax county African American owned business statistics*. Retrieved from http://www.fairfaxcountyeda.org/sites/default/files/pdf/AfricanAmericanBusinesses.pdf

Fairlie, R., & Robb, A. (2007). Why are Black-owned businesses less successful than white-owned businesses? The role of families, inheritances, and business human capital. *Journal of Labor Economics, 25*(2), 289–324.

Fairlie, R. W., & Robb, A. M. (2008). *Race and entrepreneurial success: Black-, Asian-, and White-Owned businesses in the United States.* Retrieved from http://mitpress.mit.edu/sites/default/files/titles/content/9780262514941_sch_0001.pdf

Fiedler, F. E. (1967). *A theory of leadership effectiveness.* New York, NY: McGraw-Hill.

Fink, A. (2010). *Conducting research literature reviews: From the internet to paper* (3rd ed.). Thousand Oaks, CA: SAGE Publication, Inc.

Fry, R., & Kochhar, R. (2014). *America's wealth gap between middle-income and upper-income families is widest on record.* Retrieved from http://www.pewresearch.org/fact-tank/2014/12/17/wealth-gap-upper-middle-income/

Gartner, W. B. (1985). A conceptual framework for describing the phenomenon of new venture creation. *Academy of Management Review, 10*(4), 696-706.

Gibson, S. G., Harris, M. L., Walker, P. D., & McDowell, W. C. (2014). Investigating the entrepreneurial attitudes of African Americans: A study of young adults. *The Journal of Applied Management and Entrepreneurship, 19*(2), 107-125.

Griffin, A., & Hauser, J. R. (1993). The voice of the customer. *Marketing Science, 12*(1), 1-27.

Griffith, R. (2013). *The factors that influence an entrepreneur's decision to seek formal education.* Retrieved from ProQuest Dissertation Publishing. (UMI 3597133).

Harper-Anderson, E. L. (2008). Benchmarks and barriers: African American experiences in the corporate bay area's new economy sector of the 1990s. *Journal of Planning Education and Research, 27*, 483-498.

Hennink, M., Hutter, I., & Bailey, A. (2010). *Qualitative research methods.* Thousand Oaks, CA: Sage Publications.

Hipple, S. F. (2010). *Self-employment in the United States.* Retrieved from http://www.bls.gov/opub/mlr/2010/09/art2full.pdf

Howell, J. M., & Avolio, B. J. (1993). Transformational leadership, transactional leadership, locus of control, and support for innovation: Key predictors of consolidated business-unit performance. *Journal of Applied Psychology,*

78, 891-902.

Hwang, V. W. (2012). Can entrepreneurship be taught? No: The best class is real life. *Wall Street Journal*. Retrieved from http://www.wsj.com/articles/SB10001424052970204603004577267271656000782

Inc. 5000. (2013). *Top Black entrepreneurs of 2012*. Retrieved from http://www.inc.com/ss/inc5000/abigail-tracy/top-black-entrepreneurs-2012-inc-5000

Isaksen, S. G., Dorval, K. B., & Treffinger, D. J. (2011). *Creative approaches to problem solving: A framework for innovation and change* (3rd ed.). Thousand Oaks, CA: Sage Publication Inc.

Isenberg, D. (2013). *Worthless, impossible, and stupid: How contrarian entrepreneurs create and capture extraordinary value.* Boston, MA: Harvard Business Review.

Ivy, M. (2006). *Contingency leadership among African-American male entrepreneurs: A phenomenological inquiry.* Unpublished doctoral dissertation, University of Phoenix, Phoenix, AZ.

Izquierdo E., & Buelens M. (2008). *Competing models of entrepreneurial intentions: The influence of entrepreneurial self-efficacy and attitudes*. Internationalizing Entrepreneurship Education and Training Conference, Oxford, OH.

Jacob, S. A., & Furgerson, S. P. (2012). Writing interview protocols and conducting interviews: Tip for students new to the field of qualitative research. *The Qualitative Report, 17*(6), 1-10.

Jain, T. R., Trehan, M., & Trehan, R. (2010). *Business Environment*. New Delhi, India: V. K. Entreprise.

Jim Crow Law. (2022, Jan 11). A&E Television Networks. Retrieved from www.history.com/topics/early-20th-century-us/jim-crow-laws

Johns, M. L. (2013). *Breaking the glass ceiling: Structural, cultural, and organizational barriers preventing women from achieving senior and executive positions*. Retrieved from http://www.ncbi.nlm.nih.gov/pmc/articles/PMC3544145/

Kent, T. W., Crotts, J. C., & Azziz, A. (2001). Four factors of transformational leadership behavior. *Leadership and Business Development Journal, 22*(5), 221-229.

Kinion, H. A. (2012). *Developing African American leadership in small business: A phenomenological study*. Retrieved from ProQuest Dissertation Publishing. (UMI 3538170).

Knight, F. H. (1921). *Risk, uncertainty, and profit.* New York, NY: Kelley.

Kotter, J. P. (2001). What leaders really do. *Harvard Business Review, 79*, 85-96.

Krauss, S. I., Frese, M., Friedrich, C., & Unger, J. M. (2005). Entrepreneurial orientation: A psychological model of success among southern African small business owners. *European Journal of Work and Organizational Psychology, 14*(3), 315-344.

Kumawat, H. S. (2009). *Modern entrepreneur and entrepreneurship: Theory, process and practice.* Jaipur, India: Sunrise Publishers and Distributors.

Lansley, S. (2013). *The middle class faces extinction—so does the American dream.* Retrieved from http://www.alternet.org/economy/income-inequality-defers-american-dream

Latha, K. L., & Murthy, B. E. V. V. N. (2009). The motives of small-scale entrepreneurs: An exploratory study. *South Asian Journal of Management, 16*(2), 91-108.

Lietz, C. A., Langer, C. L., & Furman, R. (2006). Establishing trustworthiness in qualitative research in social work: Implications from a study regarding spirituality. *Qualitative Social Work, 5*(4), 441-458. doi: 10.1177/14733250060702882006

Lietz, C. A., & Zayas, L. E. (2010). Evaluating qualitative research for social work practitioners. *Advances in Social Work, 11*(2), 188-202.

Lofstrom, M., & Bates, T. (2013). African Americans' pursuit of self-employment. *Small Business Economy, 40*, 73–86. doi 10.1007/s11187-011-9347-2

Lough, A. L. (2015). *Success factors for African-American entrepreneurs in North Carolina: A qualitative study.* Retrieved from ProQuest Dissertation Publishing. (UMI: 3682644).

Lumpkin, G. T., & Dess, G. G. (1996). Clarifying the entrepreneurial orientation construct and linking it to performance. *Academy of management Review, 21*(1), 135-172.

Lund Research. (2012). *Purposive sampling.* Retrieved from http://dissertation.laerd.com/purposive-sampling.php#types

Makhbul, Z. M., & Hasun, F. (2011). Entrepreneurial success: An exploratory study among entrepreneurs. *International Journal of Business and Management, 6*(1), 116-125.

Mars, M. M., & Rios-Aguilar, C. (2010). Academic entrepreneurship (re)defined: Significance and implications for the scholarship of higher education. *Journal of Higher Education and Education Planning, 59*(4), 441-460.

Mason, K. (2012). *What Causes Small Businesses to Fail?* Retrieved from http://www.moyak.com/papers/small-business-failure.html

Mason, M. (2010). Sample size and saturation in PhD studies using qualitative interviews. *Forum Qualitative Sozialforschung / Forum: Qualitative Social Research, 11*(3), Art. 8, http://nbn-resolving.de/urn:nbn:de:0114-fqs100387

Maxwell, J. A. (2013). *Qualitative research design: An interactive approach*. Thousand Oaks, CA: Sage Publications.

McClelland, C. A., (1967). *Theory of international system*. New York, NY: The MacMillan Company

McDonald-Warren, A. (2010). *Successful Black entrepreneurs in Columbia, Missouri.* Retrieved from ProQuest Digital Dissertations and Theses database. (UMI 3488822).

Mitchell, R. K., Smith, J. B., Morse, E. A., Seawright, K. W., Peredo, A., & McKenzie, B. (2002). Are entrepreneurial cognitions universal? Assessing entrepreneurial cognitions across cultures. *Entrepreneurship, Theory and Practice*, 9-32.

Momah, S. (2011). *The effect of transformational leadership: A phenomenological study of African American leadership concerns.* Retrieved from ProQuest Dissertation Publishing. (UMI 3459316).

Moustakas, C. (1994). *Phenomenological research methods.* Thousand Oaks, CA: Sage.

Murad, S. (2014). *Influence of entrepreneurial orientation on leadership styles.* Retrieved from http://essay.utwente.nl/65856/1/Murad_BA_MB.pdf

Mwasalwiba, E. S. (2010). Entrepreneurship education: A review of its objectives, teaching methods, and impact indicators. *Education & Training, 52*(1), 20-47.

National Archives. (2016). *The Emancipation Proclamation.* Retrieved from https://www.archives.gov/exhibits/featured-documents/emancipation-proclamation#:~:text=President%20Abraham%20Lincoln%20issued%20the,and%20henceforward%20shall%20be%20free.%22

National Association of School Psychologists. (2012). *Racism, prejudice, and discrimination: Position statement.* Bethesda,

MD: Author.
National Association of Social Workers. (2015). *Racism.* Retrieved from http://www.naswdc.org/pressroom/events/911/racism.asp
National Center for Education Statistics (NCES). (2014). *The condition of education 2014.* Retrieved from http://nces.ed.gov/pubs2014/2014083.pdf
National Employment Law Project. 2012. *Low-wage recovery and growing inequality*. Retrieved from http://www.nelp.org/content/uploads/2015/03/LowWageRecovery2012.pdf
Neuman, W. L. (2011). Social research methods: *Qualitative and quantitative approaches* (7th ed.). Boston, MA: Allyn and Bacon.
Newbold, K. F., & Erwin, T. D. (2014). The education of entrepreneurs: An instrument to measure entrepreneurial development. *Journal of Business & Entrepreneurship,* 141-178.
Nienaber, H. (2010). Conceptualization of management and leadership. *Management Decision, (48)*5, 661-675. doi: 10.1108/00251741011043867
Nienaber, H., & Roodt, G. (2008). Management and leadership: Buccaneering or science? *European Business Review, 20*(1), 36-50.
Northouse, P. G. (2010). *Leadership: Theory and practice* (5th ed.). Thousand Oaks, CA: Sage Publications, Inc.
Novicevic, M. N., Sloan, H., Duke, A., Holmes, E., & Breland, J. (2006). Customer relationship management: Barnard's foundation. *Journal of Management History, 12*(3), 306-318.
Ogbonna, E., & Harris, L. C. (2000). *Leadership style, organizational culture and performance: empirical evidence from UK companies*. Retrieved from http://www.hs-fulda.de/fileadmin/Fachbereich_SW/Downloads/Profs/Wolf/Studies/england_UK/uk_leadership_style.pdf
Pandey, J., & Tewary, N. B. (2011). Locus of control and achievement values of entrepreneurs. *Journal of Occupational Psychology, 52*(2), 107-111.
Parker, S. (2009). *The economics of entrepreneurship.* Cambridge, England: Cambridge University Press.
Pattie, M., Parks, L., & Wales, W. (2012). Who needs security? Entrepreneurial minorities, security values, and firm performance. *Journal of Management Inquiry, 21*(3), 319–328. doi: 10.1177/1056492611425090

Pearce, C. L., Sims, H. P. Jr., Cox, J. F., Ball, G., Schnell, E., Smith, K. A., & Trevino, L. (2003). Transactors, transformers and beyond: A multi-method development of a theoretical typology of leadership. *Journal of Management Development, 22*(4), 273-307.

Penner, J. L., & McClement, S. E. (2008). Using phenomenology to examine the experience of family caregivers of patients with advance head and neck cancer: Reflections of a novice researcher. *International Journal of Qualitative Methods, 7*(2), 92-101.

Pew Research Center (n.d.). *Businesses owned by women, minorities lag in revenue share*. Retrieved from https://www.pewresearch.org

Putta, S. S. (2014). Improving entrepreneur's management skills through entrepreneurship training. *Journal of Commerce and Management Thought, 5*(3), 459-474. doi: 10.5958/0976-478X.2014.00334.6

QSR International. (2015a). *Using NVivo for qualitative research.* Retrieved from http://help-nv10.qsrinternational.com/desktop/concepts/using_nvivo_for_qualitative_research.htm

QSR International. (2015b). *What is qualitative research*? Retrieved from http://www.qsrinternational.com/what-is-qualitative-research.aspx

Radipere, S. (2012). South African university entrepreneurship education. *African Journal of Business Management, 6*(44), 11015-11022.

Ramos-Rodriquez, A. R., Medina-Garrido, J. A., Lorenzo-Gomez, J. D., & Ruiz-Navarro, J. (2010). What you know or who you know? The role of intellectual and social capital in opportunity recognition. *International Small Business Journal, 28*(6), 566–582.

Raposo, M., & do Paço, A. (2011). Entrepreneurship education: Relationship between education and entrepreneurial activity. *Psicothema, 23*(3), 453-457.

Reardon, S. F., Bischoff, K. (2011). *Growth in the Residential Segregation of Families by income 1970-2009*. Retrieved from https://www.russellsage.org/research/reports/residential-income-segregation

Renko, M., El Tarabishy, A., Carsrud, A. L., & Brännback, M. (2015). Understanding and measuring entrepreneurial leadership style. *Journal of Small Business Management,*

53(1), 54–74. doi: 10.1111/jsbm.12086

Research Methods Knowledge Base. (2006). *Deductive and inductive*. Retrieved from http://www.socialresearchmethods.net/kb/dedind.php

Restructuring Associates. (2008). *Six step problem solving model*. Retrieved from http://www.yale.edu/bestpractices/resources/docs/problemsolvingmodel.pdf

Ricardo, D. (1817). *On the principles of political economy and taxation*. London, UK: John Murray.

Rih, N., & Guedira, M. (2014). Entrepreneurship education: Tacit knowledge and innovation transfer. *Academic Journal of Interdisciplinary Studies*

MCSER Publishing, Rome-Italy, 3(1), 253-265.

Robinson, B. B. (2014). *22 reasons why Black businesses fail*. Retrieved from www.blackeconomics.org/BELit/22REASONS.pdf

Rotter, J. B. (1966). Generalized expectancies for internal versus external control of reinforcement. *Psychological Monographs*, 80, whole no. 609.

Sánchez, J. C. (2010). University training for entrepreneurial competencies: Its impact on intention of venture creation. *International Entrepreneurship and Management Journal, April* 1-16.

Say, J. B. (1803). Traité D'économie Politique, ou Simple Exposition de la Manière Dont se Forment, se Distribuent, et se Composent les Richesses, A.A. Renouard, Paris.

Scarborough, N. M. (2012). *Effective small business management: An entrepreneurial approach* (10th ed.). Upper Saddle River, NJ: Prentice Hall.

Shapero, A. (1975). The displaced, uncomfortable entrepreneur. *Psychology Today*, November.

Sheppard, J., Jr. (2010). *Perceptions of leadership on survival of successful African-American small business owners: A phenomenological study*. Retrieved from ProQuest Dissertation Publishing. (UMI 3411122).

Shierholz, H., Sabadish, N., & Finio, N. (2013). *The class of 2013: Young graduates still face dim job prospects*. Retrieved from http://www.epi.org/publication/class-of-2013-graduates-job-prospects/

Simpeh, K. N. (2011). Entrepreneurship theories and empirical research: A summary review of the literature. *European Journal of Business and Management*

3(6), 1-9.
Singh, R. P., & Gibbs, S. R. (2013). Opportunity recognition processes of Black entrepreneurs. *Journal of Small Business & Entrepreneurship, 26*(6), 643–659. doi: 10.1080/08276331.2014.892312
Singh, R. P., Knox, E. L., & Crump, M. E. S. (2008). Opportunity recognition differences between black and white nascent entrepreneurs: A test of Bhave's model. *Journal of Developmental Entrepreneurship 13*, 59–76.
Sission, P. (2011). *The hourglass and the escalator: Labour market change and mobility*. Retrieved from http://www.theworkfoundation.com/downloadpublication/report/292_hourglass_escalator120711%20(2)%20(3).pdf
Sloan, A. & Bowe, B. (2014). Phenomenology and hermeneutic phenomenology: The philosophy, the methodologies and using hermeneutic phenomenology to investigate lecturers' experiences of curriculum design. *Quality & Quantity, 48*(3), 1291-1303.
Small Business Administration. (2014). *Small business size standards*. Retrieved from https://www.sba.gov/category/navigation-structure/contracting/contracting-officials/small-business-size-standards
Small Business Notes. (2015). *Loan approval criteria*. Retrieved from http://www.smallbusinessnotes.com/business-finances/loan-approval-criteria.html
Smith, A. (1776). *An inquiry into the nature and causes of the wealth of nations*. London, UK: Methuen Publishers.
Smith, D. A., & Tang, Z. (2013). The growth performance of top African American businesses. *Emerald Group Publishing Limited, 51*(1), 163-172. doi: 10.1108/00251741311291364
Sonfield, M., & Lussier, R. N. (2014). The influence of the entrepreneur's education level on strategic decision making. *Journal of Small Business Strategy, 24*(1), 19-28.
Starr, B. (2012). *Corporations plan for post-middle-class America*. Retrieved from http://www.huffingtonpost.com/bernard-starr/middle-class_b_1395443.html
Stogdill, R. M. (1948). Personal factors associated with leadership. *Journal of Psychology, 25*, 35–71.
Surie, G., & Ashley, A. (2008). Integrating pragmatism and ethics in entrepreneurial leadership for sustainable value creation. *Journal of Business Ethics, 81*(1), 235-246.

Taneja, S. (2010). *Entrepreneur development*. Mumbai, IND: Himalaya Publishing House.

Teleşpan, C., & Halmaghi, E. (2012). Leadership versus management. *Revista Academiei Fortelor Terestre, 17*(1), 70-73.

Thamhain, H. J. (2005). *Management of technology: Managing effectively in technology-intensive organizations*. Hoboken, NJ: John Wiley and Son.

Todd, J. (2015). *Best places for Black-owned businesses*. Retrieved from http://www.nerdwallet.com/blog/small-business/best-places-for-black-owned-businesses/

Torrance, W. (2013). Wrong question on entrepreneurship. *Inside Higher Education*. Retrieved from http://www.insidehighered.com

Truscott, D. M., Swars, S., Smith, S., Thornton-Reid, F., Zhao, Y., Dooley, C., ... Matthews, M. (2010). A cross-disciplinary examination of the prevalence of a cross-disciplinary examination of the prevalence of mixed methods in educational research in educational research: 1995–2005. *International Journal of Social Research Methodology, 13*(4), 317–328.

Tseng, C. (2013). Connecting self-directed learning with entrepreneurial learning to entrepreneurial performance. *International Journal of Entrepreneurial Behaviour & Research, 19*(4), 425-446.

Urban Institute. (2017). *Lending practices leave entrepreneurs of color on the starting block*. Retrieved from https://www.urban.org/urban-wire/lending-practices-leave-entrepreneurs-color-starting-block

U.S. Bureau of Labor Statistics. (2014). *Table A-2. Employment status of the civilian population by race, sex, and age*. Retrieved from http://www.bls.gov/news.release/empsit.t02.htm

U.S. Bureau of Labor Statistics. (2015a). *Databases, tables & calculators by subject*. Retrieved from http://data.bls.gov/pdq/SurveyOutputServlet

U.S. Bureau of Labor Statistics. (2015b). *Table A-2. Employment status of the civilian population by race, sex, and age*. Retrieved from http://www.bls.gov/news.release/empsit.t02.htm

U.S. Census Bureau. (2007). *Survey of business owners (SBO): 2007 survey results*. Retrieved from http://www.census.gov/econ/sbo/07menu.html

U.S. Census Bureau. (2010a). *The Black population: 2010.* Retrieved from http://www.census.gov/prod/cen2010/briefs/c2010br-06.pdf

U.S. Census Bureau. (2010b). *The White Population: 2010.* Retrieved from http://www.census.gov/prod/cen2010/briefs/c2010br-05.pdf

U.S. Equal Employment Opportunity Commission. (2010). *EEOC African American workgroup report.* Retrieved from http://www.eeoc.gov/federal/reports/aawg.cfm

U.S. Government Publishing Office. (2010). *Small business job act of 2010.* Retrieved from http://www.gpo.gov/fdsys/pkg/PLAW-111publ240/pdf/PLAW-111publ240.pdf

van Praag, M., van Witteloostuijn, A., & van der Sluis, J. (2013). The higher returns to formal education for entrepreneurs versus employees. *Small Business Economics, 40*(2), 375-396. doi: http://dx.doi.org/10.1007/s11187-012-9443-y

Vesper, K. A. (1980). *New venture strategies.* Englewood Cliffs, NJ: Prentice-Hall.

Vij, S., & Sharma, P. (2013). Does entrepreneurial education enhance the entrepreneurial drive of business students? *The IUP Journal of Entrepreneurship 66 Development, X*(2), 65-82.

Virginia Business. (2011). *Top 25 minority-owned businesses in Virginia.* Retrieved from http://www.virginiabusiness.com/news/article/top-25-minority-owned-businesses-in-virginia

Von Krosigk, B. (2007). A holistic exploration of leadership development. *South African Journal of Business Management, 38*(2), 25-31.

Wagner-Tsukamoto, S. (2007). An institutional economic reconstruction of scientific management: On the lost theoretical logic of Taylorism. *Academy of Management Review, 32*(1), 105-17.

Washbush, J. B. (2005). There is no such thing as leadership, revisited. *Management Decision, 43*(8), 1078-85.

Wasserman, N. (2012). Can entrepreneurship be taught? Yes: Learn about the pitfalls. *Wall Street Journal.* Retrieved from http://www.wsj.com/articles/SB10001424052970204603004577267271656000782

Wren, D. A. (2005). *The history of management thought* (5th ed.). London, UK: Wiley, John & Sons, Inc.

Xu, T., & Xu, Y. (2012). A literature review of relationship between entrepreneurial orientation and firm performance. In *Management of Technology (ISMOT), 2012 International Symposium on* (pp. 128-131). IEEE.

Yahaya, N., Taib, M. A. B. M., Ismail, J., Shariff, Z., Yahaya, A., Boon, Y., & Hashim, S. (2011). Relationship between leadership personality types and source of power and leadership styles among managers. *African Journal of Business Management, 5*(22), 9635-9648.

Yang, C. W. (2008). The relationships among leadership styles, entrepreneurial orientation, and business performance. *Managing Global Transitions*, *6*(3), 257-275.

Zafar, S., & Khan, I. M. (2014). A study of entrepreneurial success with respect to gender, education, family background, self-perceived reasons for success, and culture. *Journal of Asia Entrepreneurship and Sustainability, X*(2), 1-44.

Zhao, H., Seibert, S. E., & Lumpkin, G. T. (2010). The relationship of personality to entrepreneurial intentions and performance: A meta-analytic review. *Journal of Management, 36*(2), 381-404.

Zlomek, E. (2012). The wealth effect and college choice. *Business Week: business schools*. Retrieved from http://www.businessweek.com/articles/2012-08-03/the-wealth-effect-and-college-choice

APPENDICES

APPENDIX A

Solicitation for Dissertation Research Participation

Dear Mr. or Ms.,

I'm a doctoral candidate working on my dissertation through Argosy University. I would like to solicit your participation in my qualitative research focused on the impact of business experience and formal and informal education for successful African-American entrepreneurs in Northern Virginia. The interview is expected to take only 60-90 minutes of your time and the schedule is flexible to your availability.

The interview will include general questions that are structured to capture your personal insight on business experience and education. The information you provide will be confidential. You may decline to answer any question and you can terminate the interview at any time.

I will initiate the actual interviews circa January 2016 after the official Institutional Review Board's (IRB) approval. Meanwhile, I'm actively building my list of participants based on the selection criteria. My qualitative research will utilize the purposive sampling technique, which involve nonrandom volunteer sampling of a predefined population. The detail research criteria are as follows:

- Race - African American/Black alone or in combination with other races
- Location - Northern Virginia, which includes Washington, D.C.
- Successful entrepreneur - Full time business owner who has been an entrepreneur for a minimum of five (5) years; must be active in the decision-making of the daily business management and operations

There are two reasons for providing this study criteria information: (1) to check your qualifications and (2) my research incorporates a snowball recruitment strategy. The snowball recruitment strategy simply involves asking the study participant to refer other participants who meet the study criteria.

Contact Dr. Grace Klinefelter (Doctoral Dissertation Research Chair) if you would like additional information in reference to your participation. I sincerely appreciate if you would send me a brief email to confirm your participation status and any referrals you would be kind enough to recommend.

Kind regards,
Edward L. Wiggins, III, Doctoral Candidate
Argosy University

APPENDIX B

Consent Form

You are invited to participate in a phenomenological study on the impact of leadership experience and the acquisition of education for successful African American entrepreneurs in Northern Virginia. You were selected as a potential participant base on the qualification criteria. Read this informed consent form, as it is part of the process, to allow you to understand this study before deciding to take part. Edward L. Wiggins, a doctoral student at Argosy University, is conducting this study.

Background Information:

The purpose of this qualitative phenomenological study is to explore the impact of leadership experience and the acquisition of education for successful African American entrepreneurs in Northern Virginia.

Procedures:

If you consent to being in this study, you will asked to:

- Interview face-to-face not to exceed 90 minutes
- Interview at a mutually agreed data and time
- Allow research to take notes and use audio recording device during interview
- Review researcher's written summation for accuracy

Interview Sample questions:

1. What was your level of business experience entering into business?
2. What was your level of education entering into business?

Voluntary Nature of the Study:

Your participation in this study is voluntary. Your decision on whether or not to participate in this study will be respected by everyone. If your decision is to participate, you can at your own free will refuse to answer any questions or withdraw from the interview at any time.

Risk and Benefits of Being in the Study:

There is no associated risk to your safety and well-being for participating in this study. This research is designed to provide successful African-American entrepreneurs' insight on the area of leadership experience and formal and informal education.

Compensation:

There is no compensation for your participation in this study.

Confidentiality:

The information you provide will be kept confidential. The researcher will not include your name or company's name that will identify you. The collected data will be password protected and/or secured in a locked storage accessible only by the researcher.

Audio Recording:

An audio recording device will be used to accurately capture your responses. You have the right to refuse the interview from being recorded without penalty. Please initial one of the following options:

I consent to audio recording:

Yes______ No______

Contacts and Questions:

You may ask any questions you have for clarity and understanding. You can contact me via telephone at XXX-XXX-XXXX or email at edward_wiggins@email if you have questions later. If you have questions in regards to your privacy, you can contact the Doctoral Dissertation Research Chair, Dr. Grace Klinefelter, via gklinefelter@email or XXX-XXX-XXXX.

Statement of Consent:

I have read the consent information above. I have asked questions and received answers to clarify my understanding. I agree to the terms within this document, and I consent to participate in this study.

Printed Name of Participant:

____

Date of Consent:

____

Signature of Participant:

____

Signature of Researcher:

____

APPENDIX C

Interview Questions

Date/Time: ____________

Demographic Information

Industry: ______________________

Participant #: ____________________

Race: __________________________

Yrs. in Business: ________________

Gender: ________________________

Location (City, State): _____________

Age: ___________________________

Number of Employees: ____________

Business Role: __________________

Avg. Annual Gross Receipts*: $______

Ownership (Sole Proprietor, Corp., Partnership, or Other): ____________

Were your parents entrepreneurs?

____

If so, what type of business?

____

What was your level of **formal education entering into business? _______________________________

Interview Questions

1. Describe what motivated you to become an entrepreneur.
2. Did you own any businesses prior to your current business? If so, how many years of business experience did you have prior to your current business?
3. What was your leadership background entering into your current business?
4. Describe the business experience you had to gain to remain competitive in business.
5. Describe how you developed your leadership to remain competitive in business.
6. What challenges or obstacles did you encounter entering into business? How did you overcome these challenges or obstacles?
7. In your opinion, what are the most important entrepreneurial characteristics for success in business?
8. Describe the formal education** you had to acquire to remain competitive in business.
9. How was formal education instrumental to your business success?
10. Describe the informal education*** you had to

acquire to sustain your business.

11. How was informal education instrumental to your business success?
12. Would you share any other business experiences that would be relevant to this study?
13. What advice would you have for others considering entrepreneurship?

Notes:

*__Avg. Annual Gross Receipts__ – Based on the years in your current business

**__Formal education__ – Acquired through infrastructures that validate a level of proficiency. A formal education infrastructure can be an accredited college or certified training institution.

***__Informal education__ - Informal education does not have organized accreditation or certification curriculums. Knowledge acquired from informal education can be sourced through the conventional means of seminars, professional literature, internet, and other practical applications (i.e., scientific or didactic games, lectures, case studies, discussions) of updating knowledge base.

APPENDIX D

Transcriber Confidentiality Agreement

I, ______________________________, will have access to confidential information, which is not disclosed. I acknowledge the information provided by Edward L. Wiggins must remain confidential and the improper disclosure of confidential information can be damaging to the participants in the study. This confidential information is provide to me for the sole purpose of transcribing the data.

I acknowledge and agree to the following terms and conditions:

1. I will not disclose or discuss any confidential information with others, including friends or family.

2. I will not in any way share, copy, release, sell, loan, alter, or destroy any confidential information except as properly authorized.

3. I will not make any unauthorized transmissions, inquiries, modifications, or purging of confidential information.

4. I agree that my obligations under this agreement will continue after completion of the transcription duties.

5. I understand that violation of this agreement could have legal implications.

6. I will transcribe the recorded information to the best of my ability, and I will not willingly leave any information out of the transcribed materials.

Date of Agreement:

____

Signature of Transcriber:

____

INDEX

ABOUT THE AUTHOR

Dr. Edward L. Wiggins, III, is a retired veteran with over 21 years in the U.S. Army as a Communication, Electronic, and Signals Intelligence Expert.

He has facilitated curriculum for various universities as a professor teaching Information Technology, Project Management, Information Systems, and business courses.

Dr. Wiggins currently serves as a Strategic Business Advisor supporting the Department of Defense (DoD), U.S. Federal Government, and corporate industry in the areas of Portfolio/Program Management.

Dr. Wiggins has a Doctor of Business Administration with an emphasis in Management, a Master of Business Administration with a concentration in Acquisition and Procurement, and a Bachelor of Science in Management Computer Information Systems.

He enjoys vintage automotive restoration, woodwork, skiing, golf, reading, listening to jazz music, and spending time with family.

ORBIS NOVITAS SOLUTIONS, INC.

https://orbisnovitas.com/

Orbis Novitas Solutions, Inc. is a Management Consulting firm. Our business emphases are in Education and Training, Business Management, and Information Technology.

Orbis Novitas Solutions, Inc., provides quality consulting services driven to augment innovative business solutions for the Department of Defense, U.S. Government, and commercial industry. We focus on process improvement to mitigate risk. Our purpose is to enhance the customers' ability to accomplish its mission/goals through measurable and repeatable processes.

Orbis Novitas Solutions, Inc. optimizes the customers' ability to accomplish strategic goals. We take pride in delivering high-quality management and technical consulting services to businesses that simply need to know how to proceed in today's economy. Our globalized economy is fueled by technology-enhanced capabilities, which create business environments that require the ability to rapidly respond to the changing demands of the consumer and governing policies.

ABOUT THE BOOK

Academic literature has historically provided reasons why African-American entrepreneurs failed in business. Minimal research evidence existed on successful African American entrepreneurs' proven business characteristics, traits, and practices. There are African-American entrepreneurs who have established successful businesses despite centuries of discrimination that led to the social impacts of access to capital, limited business experience, and entrepreneurial knowledge.

This book shares the business experience of 21 successful African-American entrepreneurs who contributed empirical solutions to the problems business owners will contend with in business. This book is a must read for nascent and novice entrepreneurs, entrepreneurs working to overcoming or avoid business obstacles, researchers interested in contributing more solutions in the entrepreneurial arena.

The literature review, data processing and analysis, and emerging themes will infuse the reader with key business considerations, new ideas, and approaches to navigate the inherent business pitfalls thereby increase your business success.

www.ingramcontent.com/pod-product-compliance
Lightning Source LLC
LaVergne TN
LVHW051236080426
835513LV00016B/1610
* 9 7 8 1 9 4 8 1 4 9 1 9 8 *